Studios & **Workshops**
Spaces for Creatives

Sibylle Kramer

Studios &
Workshops
Spaces for Creatives

BRAUN

CONTENTS

6 Preface

Designing Spaces

12 **Out of Office**
KNOL

16 **Daxing Factory Conversion**
Tsutsumi & Associates
Nie Yong

20 **Studio in the Woods**
selgascano

24 **Onesize**
Origins Architecture

28 **21 Cake Headquarters**
People's Architecture Office

32 **Assemble Studio**
Assemble Studio

36 **Studio R**
studio mk27
Marcio Kogan + Gabriel Kogan

42 **Brandbase Pallet Project**
MOST Architecture

46 **Kirchplatz Office**
Oppenheim Architecture + Design Europe
Huesler Architekten

50 **Beats By Dre**
Bestor Architecture

56 **BICOM Offices**
Jean de Lessard, creative designers

60 **Halle A**
Designliga

64 **The Green Studio**
Fraher Architects

68 **Jung von Matt Headquarters**
Stephen Williams Associates

72 **The Workshop Behind The Scenes**
Eriksen Skajaa Architects

Thinking Together

78 **SoundCloud Headquarters**
KINZO Berlin

82 **Flamingo Shanghai Office – The Attic**
Neri&Hu Design and Research Office

86 **SKA Studio**
SKA Sibylle Kramer Architekten

90 **Headvertising Offices**
Corvin Cristian

94 **UWSA bikeLAB**
Peter Sampson Architecture Studio

98 **Ajando Next Level CRM**
Peter Stasek Architects – Corporate Architecture

102 **Panic, Inc.**
Holst Architecture

106 **Cisco**
Studio O+A

110 **De Burgemeester**
Studioninedots

114 **Superheroes**
Simon Bush-King Architecture & Urbanism

118 **Particular Studio**
Particular

122 **One Workplace Showroom and Headquarters**
Design Blitz

126 **Nova Iskra Design Incubator**
Petokraka

130 **Kantoor IMD**
Ector Hoogstad Architecten

134 **HOME4 Designstudio**
Hadi Teherani AG
Hadi Teherani Interior GmbH

Meeting People

140 Ansarada Office Those Architects	**188 HDG Architecture's Office** HDG Architecture	**230 BBDO Group** Boris Voskoboinikov
144 FINE Design Group Boora Architects	**192 3Logic MK Corporate HQ** nuvolaB architetti associati	**234 Nasty Gal Headquarters** Bestor Architecture
148 MAD Office DOS Architects	**196 Innovation Center** SCOPE office for architecture	**238 Archway Studios** Undercurrent Architects
152 Workshop in the Attic PL.ARCHITEKCI	**Building Concepts**	**242 Pixiv Office** TeamLab Architect
156 Covus sbp – Seel Bobsin Partner	**202 Dynabyte** pS Arkitektur	**246 Hadi Teherani Headquarters** Hadi Teherani AG Hadi Teherani Interior GmbH
160 Analog Folk DH Liberty	**206 ICRAVE Office** ICRAVE	**250 Pride and Glory Interactive Head Office** Morpho Studio
164 Birkenstock Australia Headquarters Melbourne Design Studios	**210 Giraldi Associates Architects Headquarters** GIRALDI ASSOCIATES ARCHITECTS	**254 V-Confession Agency Office** Architectural studio M17
168 Studio – Showroom & Gallery estudio ji (Jorge Frías + Irene Zurdo)	**214 Zeit Online Editorial** de Winder Architects	**258 Unit B4 Office** MAKE Creative
172 FiftyThree +ADD	**218 Uniform** Snook Architects	264 Architects' Index
176 Path Offices GEREMIA DESIGN	**222 Nudie Jeans Headquarters** Okidoki arkitekter	270 Picture Credits
180 Wordpress Automattic Space Baran Studio Architecture	**226 Komdat** Reaktioneins Guido Meier Ralf Bender Design	272 Imprint
184 Giant Pixel Studio O+A		

PREFACE

Studios & Workshops
by Sibylle Kramer

They're still to be found, those neatly plotted office spaces with the economically calculated areas and standard furnishings according to the specified minimum requirements. But creative work has other requirements and uses other standards to create completely different environs which are an inspiration, giving ideas the space they need, far beyond norms and standards. "Studios & Workshops" shows rooms where work is being done which are by no means similar. In ways that have little to do with the usual offices they offer comfort and encouragement to linger. The design concepts of the architects and designers are guided by the creative needs of their occupants. Open common areas are laid out for communication and feedback, while specially shaped zones and niches provide the opportunity to withdraw for concentration and a more introverted mode of thought. The concepts are as different as what is being created in these workshops. Expansive common areas are left in their original charming industrial condition, cosily designed or in stark contrast to the otherwise familiar work setting. Work islands, conference rooms or relaxation zones are implanted inside the common areas as a kind of house-within-a-house, as spatial sculptor or cocoons. Or as rows of identical work cells. "Work hard, play hard", could be the motto of many of the studios and workshops shown here, and again and again one finds furniture and elements that belong more to after-hours or vacation spots. Instead of the trusty swivel chair, staging with a bed complete with bed covers, a rocking chair in the green room or a comfortable armchair have been

PREFACE

installed. Well equipped kitchens, rooms for ping-pong or billiards establish an atmosphere of relaxation that is conducive to communication as the basis for intensive and creative output. The spatial designs in this book range from light-purist, like the Daxing Factory Conversion project by the studio Tsutsumi & Associates, to the low budget rough, like the convincingly converted Euro palette installation by Most Architecture with their project Brandbase Pallet Project. Concepts that are rigorously followed through, high value materials and the finer details create freedom and inspire, as the Neri&Hu Design and Research Office with the Flamingo Shanghai Office or the Stephen Williams Associates Jung von Matt Headquarters in Hamburg demonstrate in spectacular ways. Look over the creative shoulders of individuals in the other office worlds of "Studios & Workshops".

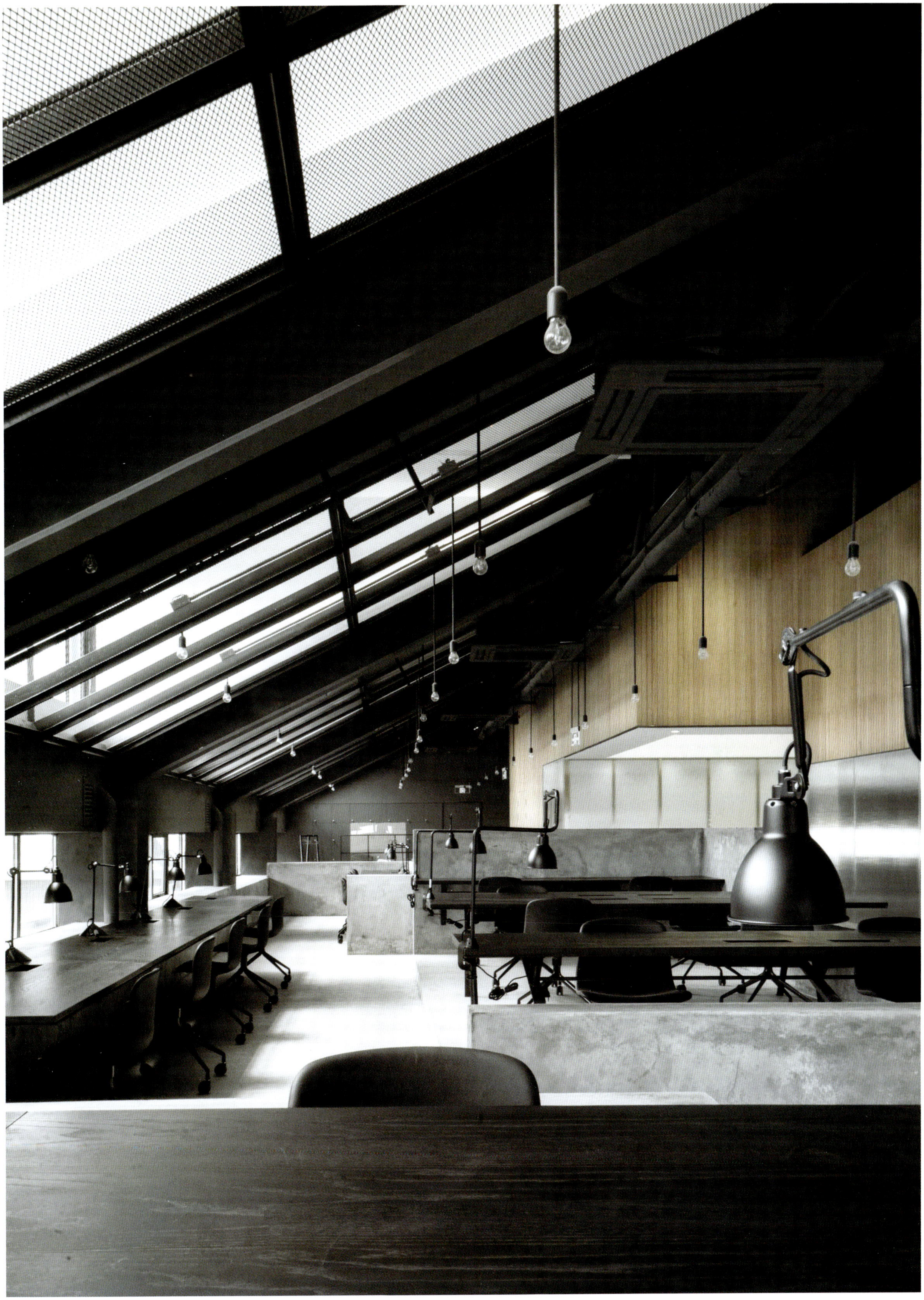

DESIGNING SPACES

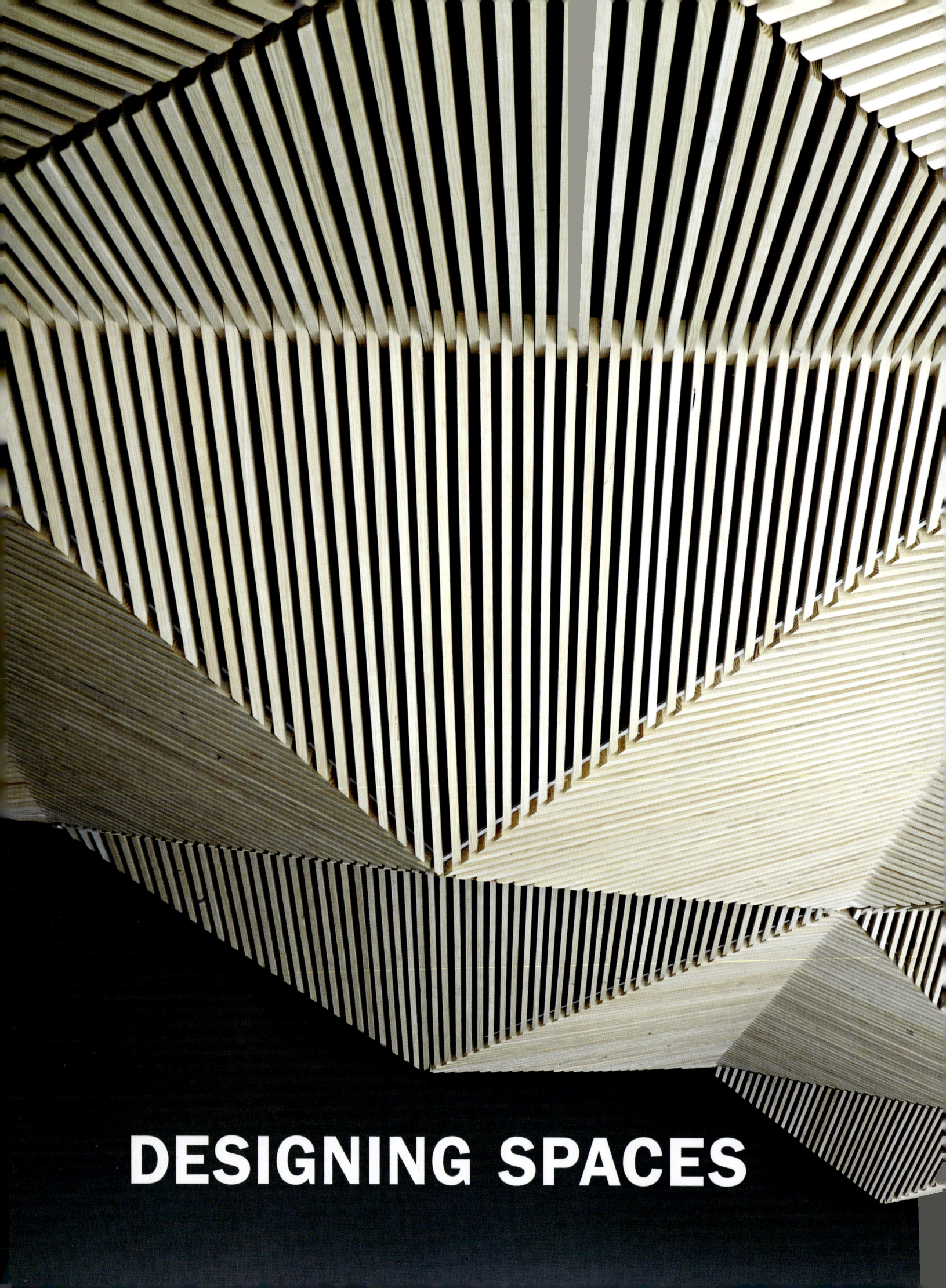

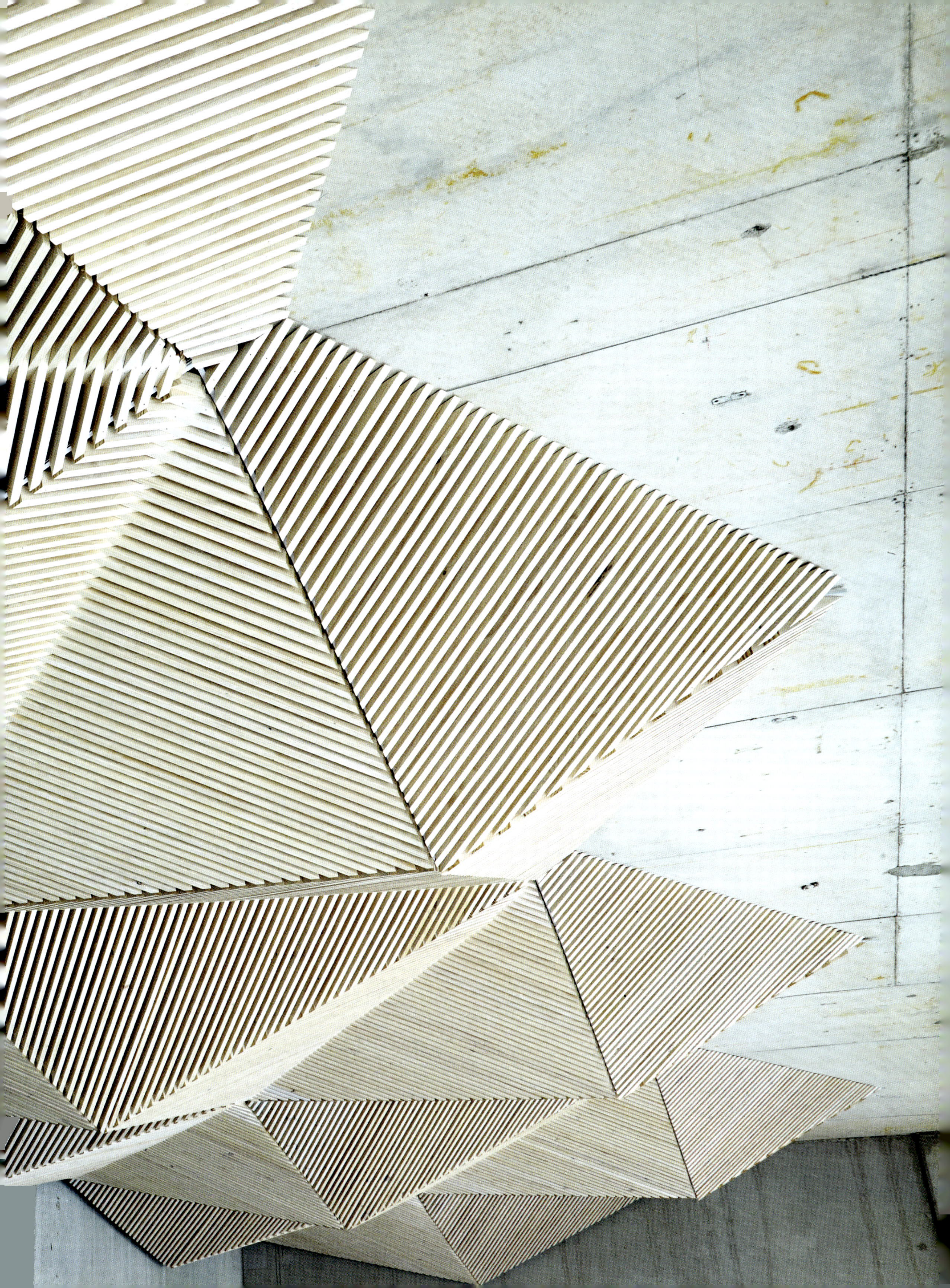

DESIGNING SPACES | KNOL

↑ | Swing & office rabbit
↗ | Bed
→ | Interior view

Out of Office

Eindhoven

In early April 2014, the ideal flexworking space Out of Office was established in Eindhoven. It is a place that fits the work ethic of the 21st century. At least, supposedly, because over the course of one month, it transformed from a playful workspace with a swing, a cuddly office rabbit and a bed, into a space with a disciplined grid of gray cubicles and strict rules. The flexworkers were unaware of this social-architectural experiment that critically reflects on the hype of new, flexible way of working. From Out of Office, KNOL simply went back to office, wondering, what really 'works'?

PROJECT FACTS

Location: Emmasingel 20, Eindhoven, The Netherlands. **Interior co-designer:** Christiaan Bakker. **Social setup and research:** Anna Dekker. **Client:** MU Eindhoven. **Completion:** 2014. **Gross floor area:** 300 m². **Type of business:** flexwork space / exhibition.

DESIGNING SPACES   KNOL

↑ | Interior view
← | Conference desk

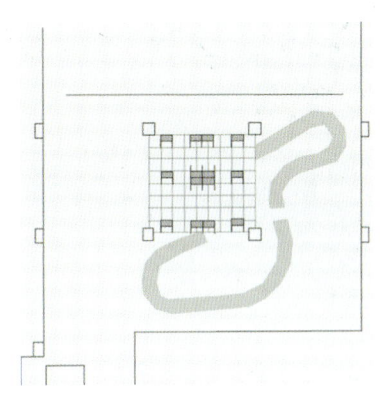

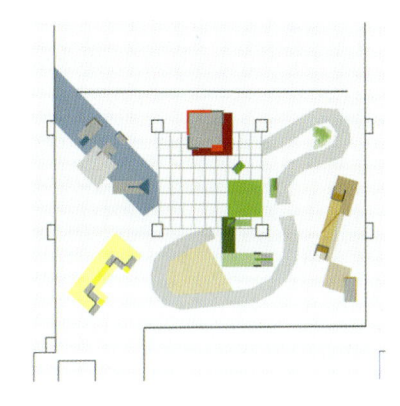

OUT OF OFFICE 15

← | Interior view
↑ | Floor plans
↓ | Flexworker desks

DESIGNING SPACES

Tsutsumi & Associates – Nie Yong

↑ | **Meeting space**
↓ | **Office area,** communication between each level

↓ | **General view,** meeting space between offices and entrance hall
→ | **Spiral staircase**

Daxing Factory Conversion

Beijing

The factory building was converted to house the head office of the furniture manufacturer. The factory occupies the first and second floors, and half of third floor, with the other half of the third floor devoted to exhibition space. The office space is on the fourth floor. The third floor exhibition space is connected to the fourth floor with spiral stairs where the existing floor was removed. The 5.5-meter ceiling height is enough for a skip-floor style to realize a three-dimensional office landscape. Office space was planned to be open, with the closed rooms treated as a group of several volumes within the huge space. The landscape has various levels, with white boxes placed to form a village. There are bypasses, hidden and open areas, an alcove with a view of the atrium, and an overview of the whole area from the loft space.

PROJECT FACTS **Location:** Qing Yun Dian, Daxing, Beijing, China. **Design team:** Nie Yong, Zhang Lei. **Client:** THT Design & Consulting. **Completion:** 2013. **Gross floor area:** 4,964 m². **Type of business:** furniture manufacturer.

DESIGNING SPACES   TSUTSUMI & ASSOCIATES – NIE YONG

↑ | Meeting space
← | Spiral staircase
↓ | Floor plans

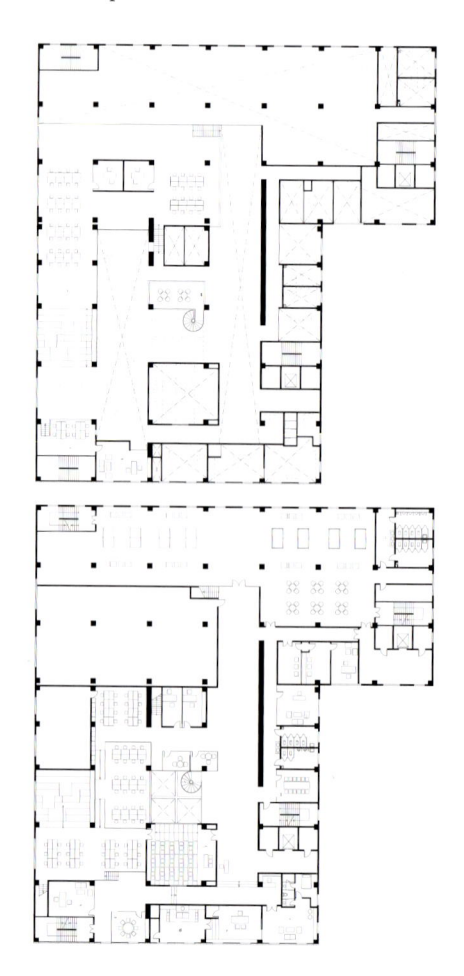

DAXING FACTORY CONVERSION

← | Spiral in the void
↓ | Open office space

DESIGNING SPACES | selgascano

↑ | **Exterior view,** studio in the woods
→ | **Interior view,** people working

Studio in the Woods

Madrid

The idea of this studio is quite simple: work under the trees. To do that a roof is required that is as transparent as possible. At the same time, the desk zone must be isolated from direct sunlight. Hence the transparent northern section that is covered with a bent sheet of 20-millimeter-colorless plexiglas. The south side, where the desks are, has to be closed in much more, but not completely, so there is double sheet of fiberglass and polyester in its natural color on the south side, with translucent insulation in the middle. Together they form a 110-millimeter-thick sandwich. In the former case, the view to the rear is clear and transparent. The view is translucent, somewhat blurred by the cantilevered metal structure left inside the sandwich, with the shadow of the trees projecting onto it gently.

PROJECT FACTS **Location:** Madrid, Spain. **Client:** private. **Completion:** 2009. **Gross floor area:** 80 m². **Type of business:** architecture studio.

DESIGNING SPACES	SELGASCANO

↑ | Exterior view
← | Sections

STUDIO IN THE WOODS

↑ | Night view
← | Entrance area

DESIGNING SPACES | Origins Architecture

↑ | **Office,** interior view
↓ | **3D schemes**

↗ | **Projection room**
→ | **Meeting space**

Onesize

Amsterdam

Smack bang in the middle of a spacious, industrial warehouse on the outskirts of Amsterdam, an intriguing object houses the Onesize studio, with dark rooms for film projection as the central meeting point. Instead of the usual location on the periphery of an office, Origins' founder Jamie van Lede placed the dark rooms centrally to indicate the nature of the firm's work. The rest of the program lines the edge of the space. It was not only the firm's line of work that provided inspiration. The visual modeling that is done in the studio inspired Origins Architecture to make an object with a minimum of polygons, transforming the program into an interesting shape while simultaneously subdividing the space for a clear routing.

PROJECT FACTS **Location:** Amsterdam, The Netherlands. **Designer:** Origins Architecture. **Contractor:** KNE+. **Client:** Onesize Motion Graphics. **Completion:** 2011. **Gross floor area:** 300 m². **Type of business:** motion graphics.

25

DESIGNING SPACES   ORIGINS ARCHITECTURE

ONESIZE

←← | Meeting space
↑ | Workspace
← | Interior view, office
↓ | Floor plan and section

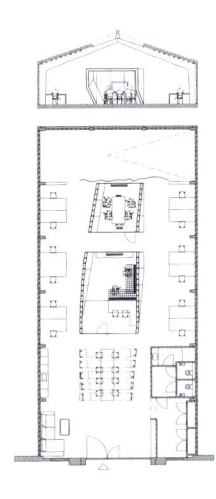

DESIGNING SPACES | People's Architecture Office

↑ | **Staircase**
→ | **Atrium,** from 2nd floor

21 Cake Headquarters

Beijing

The design for the headquarters of 21 Cake, a popular gourmet cake franchise, relies on the interaction of the three primary colors: red, yellow and blue. Selected walls of the office, namely those along circulation areas, are made of laminated colored glass. These glass panels of primary colors are layered to create a full spectrum of changing colors. As one walks through the spaces of the office, changing vantage points in combination with natural and artificial light and reflections produce dramatic effects. A double-height central atrium topped with a skylight brings in light through the layers of color along the staircase and glass bridge on the second floor. Conference tables and mobile work tables are designed and produced by People's Industrial Design Office, a sister company of the designer.

PROJECT FACTS **Location:** Legend town creative industry park, Ciyunsi bridge, Chaoyang district, Beijing, China. **Client:** 21 Cake. **Completion:** 2012. **Gross floor area:** 457 m². **Type of business:** retailer.

DESIGNING SPACES   PEOPLE'S ARCHITECTURE OFFICE

21 CAKE HEADQUARTERS

←← | **Office area**, under the atrium
↑ | **Interior view**, stained glass
↙ | **Floor plans**

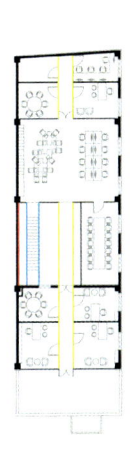

DESIGNING SPACES | Assemble Studio

↑ | Experimental ceiling design
→ | Interior view

Assemble Studio

Northcote

Assemble designed their own studio in Northcote. The aim was to create a low-cost, flexible workspace that would be an inspiring workplace. As a company with design at its core, it was important for the office to use the studio as a kind of three-dimensional showcase for their design capabilities and sensibility. Assemble Studio negotiated the design and construction through an organic process in which the design and detailing of the fit-out were improved upon and adapted as the build progressed. The ceiling design grew out of a process of experimentation, folding different sculpted origami forms in paper. The eventual design was composed of five triangles mirrored and repeated eight times across the length of the ceiling. All the custom-built furniture in the studio is on castor wheels so it can easily be shifted and the space reconfigured for events and design workshops.

PROJECT FACTS

Location: 20 High Street, Northcote, Australia. **Completion:** 2010. **Gross floor area:** 100 m². **Type of business:** architecture, design and property development company focused on small footprint projects.

DESIGNING SPACES ASSEMBLE STUDIO

ASSEMBLE STUDIO

35

←← | Interior view
↑ | Custom-built furniture
← | Floor plan and schematic drawing

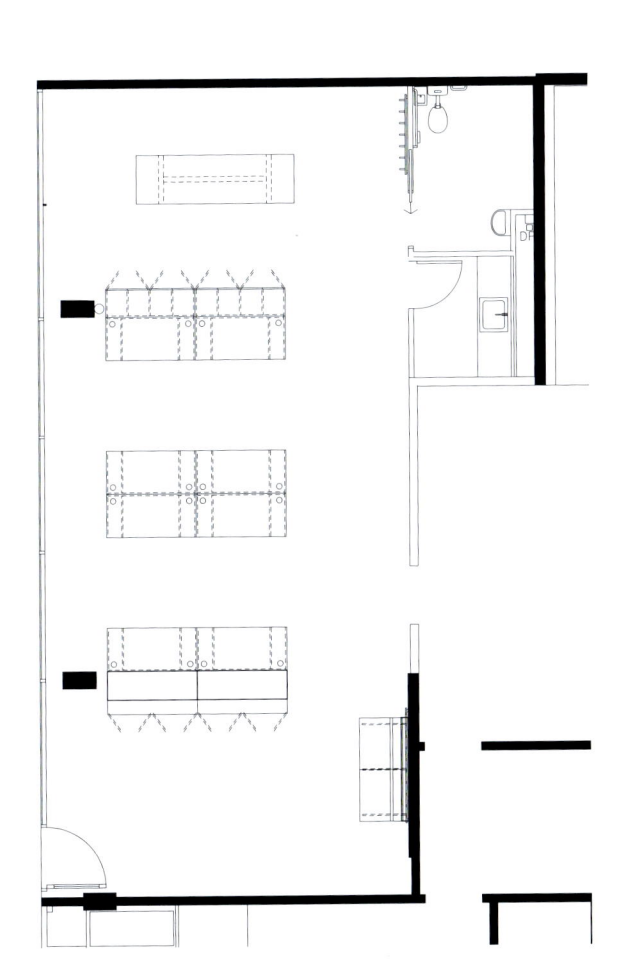

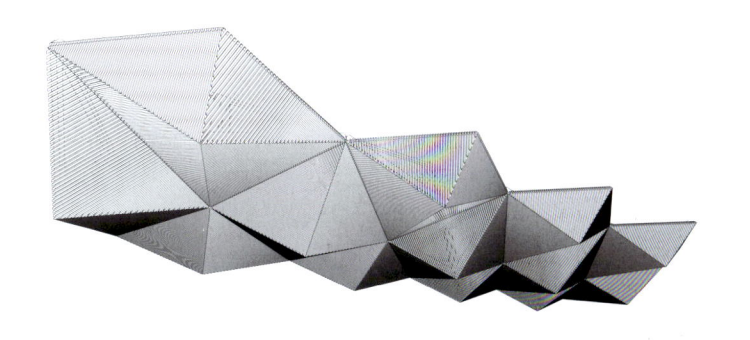

DESIGNING SPACES | studio mk27 – Marcio Kogan + Gabriel Kogan

↑ | Exterior view
↗ | Flow between gardens and studio space
→ | Open studio space

Studio R

São Paulo

Facing a small urban square, the loft studio opens entirely to the outside. The inner space of this photography studio flows into the side gardens of the building and the surrounding urban space, establishing a spatial continuity between the square and the building. The façade, an aluminum gate, is recessed into the concrete binding, integrating the front patio with the square; in addition two large swinging metal gates permit flow between the gardens and the open space of the studio. When they are opened, all visual barriers between internal and external space disappear. When closed, they allow the light in the photography studio to be controlled artificially. The material used in the interior displays an industrial esthetic, appropriate for the intensive use of a photography studio that needs to constantly transform itself, depending on the situation.

PROJECT FACTS **Location:** São Paulo, Brazil. **Contractor:** Lock Engenharia. **Client:** private. **Completion:** 2012. **Gross floor area:** 373 m². **Type of business:** photography studio.

DESIGNING SPACES STUDIO MK27 – MARCIO KOGAN + GABRIEL KOGAN

↑ | Interior view
← | Makeup room

STUDIO R

↑ | **Office**
← | **Detail**, perforated façade
↓ | **Section and ground floor plan**

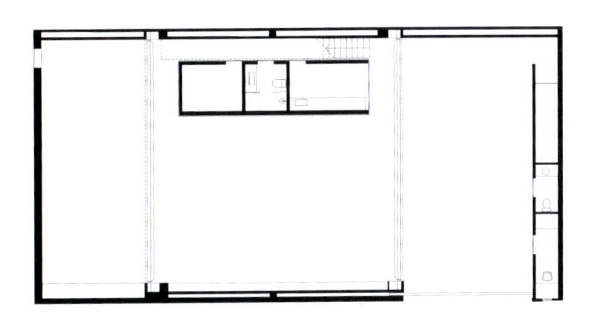

DESIGNING SPACES   STUDIO MK27 – MARCIO KOGAN + GABRIEL KOGAN

↑ | Exterior view
← | Roof terrace

STUDIO R 41

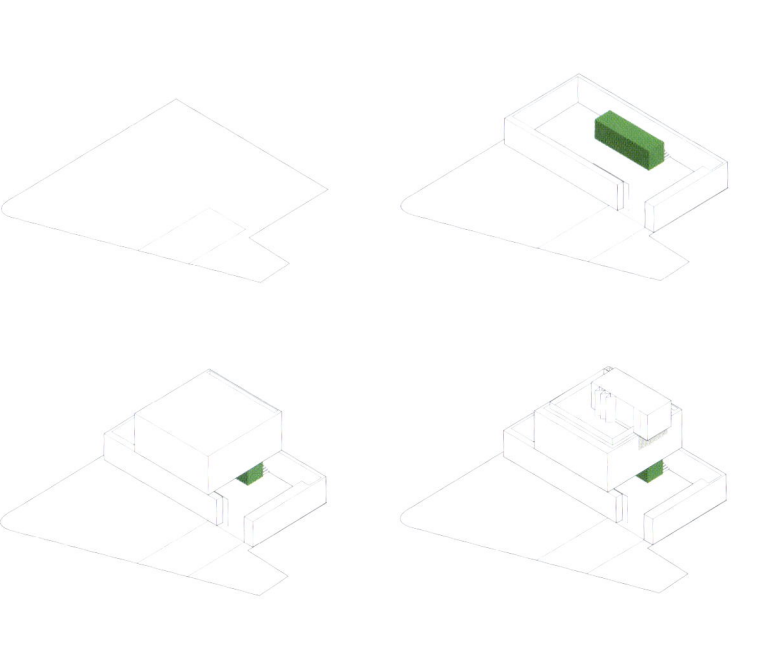

← | Staircase
↑ | 3D schemes
↓ | Office

DESIGNING SPACES | MOST Architecture

↑ | **The boardroom,** desks of the management premises
↗ | **Design studio,** cable bundles hanging like lianas
→ | **Main section**

Brandbase Pallet Project

Amsterdam

Temporary furnishing for the new office location combined with the explicit wish to outfit the space with an authentic, recyclable material, gave creative director Marvin Pupping and MOST Architecture the idea to use Euro-pallets for this particular design. The pallet structure allows for an open, autonomous landscape that gradually changes its character, facilitating all parts of the office. The pallet structure is not designed to be a mere workplace; the entire arrangement invites you to stand, sit or lay down on the pallets. This open office concept was created to suit a creative advertising agency, with an additional, informal atmosphere.

| **PROJECT FACTS** **Location:** Amsterdam, The Netherlands. **Creative director:** Marvin Pupping. **Client:** Brandbase. **Completion:** 2013. **Gross floor area:** 245 m². **Type of business:** advertising agency.

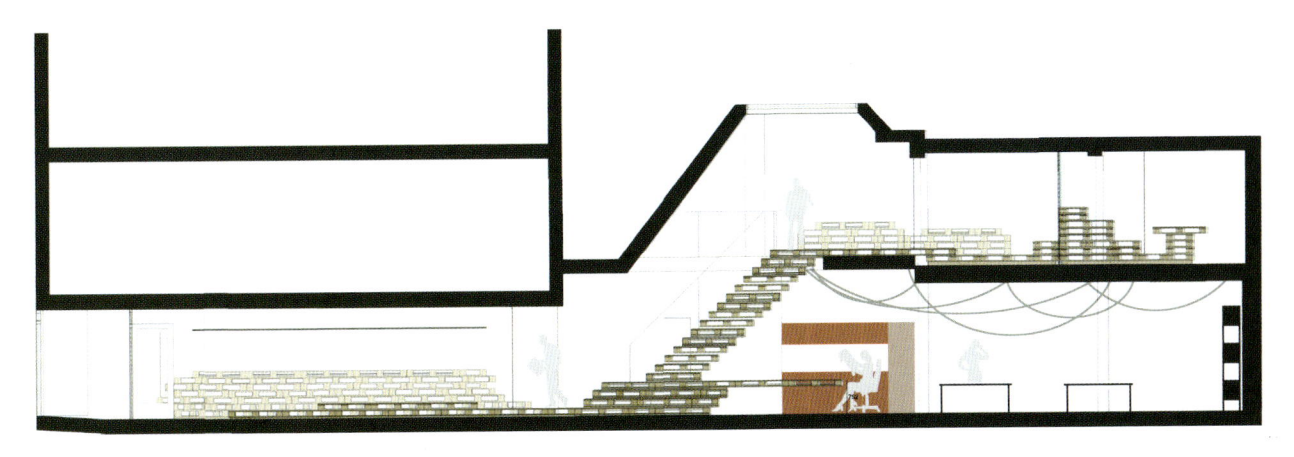

DESIGNING SPACES   MOST ARCHITECTURE

BRANDBASE PALLET PROJECT

↖↖ | View from the lunchtable
↙↙ | View of the stair balustrade
← | Meeting room
↓ | Plan diagrams

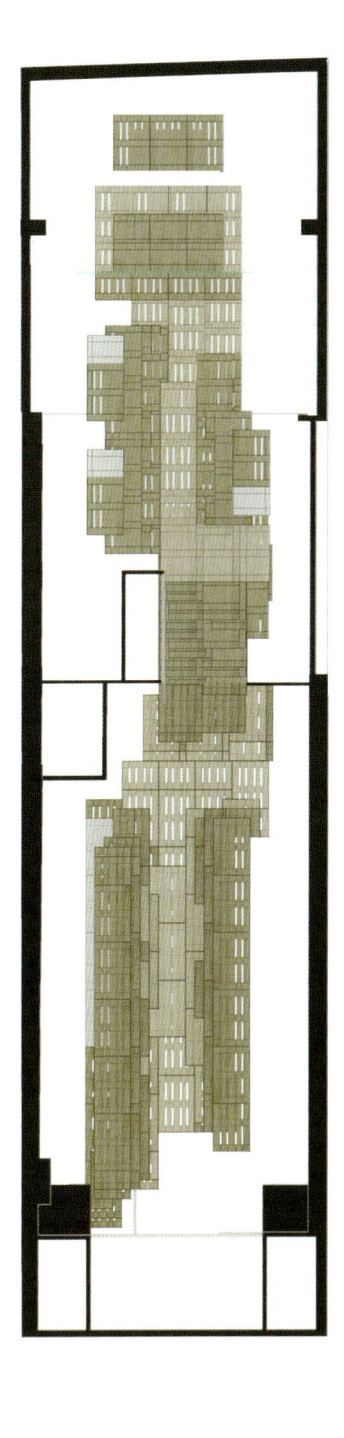

DESIGNING SPACES | Oppenheim Architecture + Design Europe
Huesler Architekten

↑ | Exterior view
↗ | Interior view
→ | Gallery

Kirchplatz Office

Basel

In 2007 the community had no more need of the space and wanted to sell the property. The submission by OAD / Huesler Architekten won the contract in an open architectural competition. The firm then took over the property according to building law and realized the project. It envisions building a studio in an outbuilding, two two-story apartments in the main building and the construction of a free-standing apartment building on the location of the shed in the rear. Today the large central opening of the threshing floor gate provides a glimpse into the spaciously extended multi-purpose room, which is available for use by the community, the church or for private occasions. The touchy question of the illumination of the studio rooms on five levels of the barn was solved by installing new openings inside where they make sense.

PROJECT FACTS **Location:** Kirchplatz 18, 4132 Muttenz, Basel, Switzerland. **Client:** STWE K18, 4132 Muttenz. **Completion:** 2011. **Gross floor area:** 330 m². **Type of business:** architecture atelier.

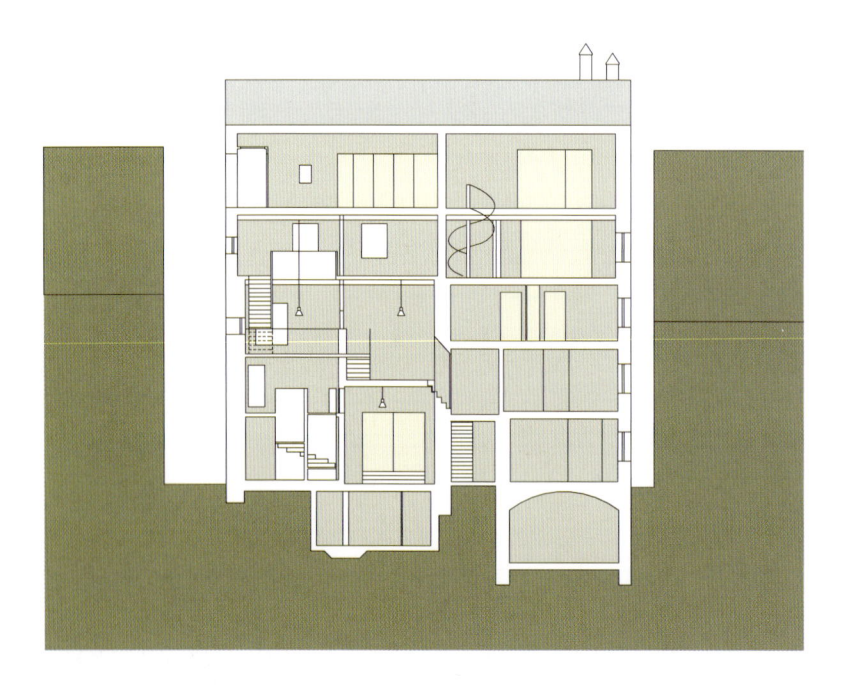

DESIGNING SPACES   OPPENHEIM ARCHITECTURE + DESIGN EUROPE / HUESLER ARCHITEKTEN

↑ | Workspace
← | Cross section

KIRCHPLATZ OFFICE

49

← | Staircase
↑ | Ground floor plan
↓ | Atelier

DESIGNING SPACES | Bestor Architecture

↑ | **Blue courtyard**
↗ | **Red hallways,** connect courtyards to cafe
→ | **White conference room**

Beats By Dre

Culver City

Beats by Dre had grown rapidly and needed more than a traditional office to accommodate their innovative research, design, and development. They needed a campus that connected and integrated these parts. Bestor Architecture designed the adaptive reuse of a three-building campus for the company, which is based in Culver City. The hub area respects the global nature of the business by creating an open contemporary luxurious lounge, allowing frequently travelling employees a spot to work in comfort. Zones of individual workstations (some with standing tables) are punctuated with break out spaces and elegant and playful architectural elements, allowing for maximum flexibility and the continual growth of teams. Daylight is brought into the entire campus via industrial roof monitors, which greatly reduce the energy load for the complex.

| **PROJECT FACTS** | **Location:** Culver City, California, USA. **Workplace and technical consultant:** Loescher + Meachem Architects. **Client:** Beats By Dre. **Completion:** 2014. **Gross floor area:** 9,752 m². **Type of business:** electronics and music streaming. |

DESIGNING SPACES BESTOR ARCHITECTURE

↑ | **Brainstorming corners,** are cut out for team meetings
← | **Building 2,** with Iwan Baan aerial

BEATS BY DRE

← | **Conference room,** view across the blue courtyard
↓ | **Connecting area,** for group sessions

DESIGNING SPACES BESTOR ARCHITECTURE

← | **Central lobby,** with mirrored wall
↓ | **Blue courtyard,** with project room to left

BEATS BY DRE

← | **Conference room,** custom wallpaper by Bestor Architecture
↓ | **Entry lobby,** waiting area

DESIGNING SPACES | Jean de Lessard, creative designers

↑ | **Closed office**
→ | **Entrance area**

BICOM Offices

Montréal

When entering the new offices of BICOM Communications, one is immediately struck by the positive energy they radiate. This feeling of positive energy is the main interior design theme that concerns the "communicator" aspect of a place where large public relations campaigns are devised. Jean de Lessard chose the archetype of the small house, because it brings out emotions that trigger happy memories at the summer cottage by the lake and campfires at night. Despite the rigidity of the construction materials used to build them, the cottages employ a flexible design system that allows growth within the agency. As a core element contributing to the well-being of the team, de Lessard has created a micro village where the effervescent environment becomes a factor supporting accomplishment and evolution for the individual and the community.

| PROJECT FACTS | **Location:** 5425 rue Casgrain, Montréal, Québec, Canada. **Client:** BICOM Communications. **Completion:** 2013. **Gross floor area:** 418 m². **Type of business:** public relations agency.

DESIGNING SPACES   JEAN DE LESSARD, CREATIVE DESIGNERS

↑ | **Open space office**
← | **Lounge space**

BICOM OFFICES

↑ | Interior view, office
← | Conference room
↓ | Floor plan

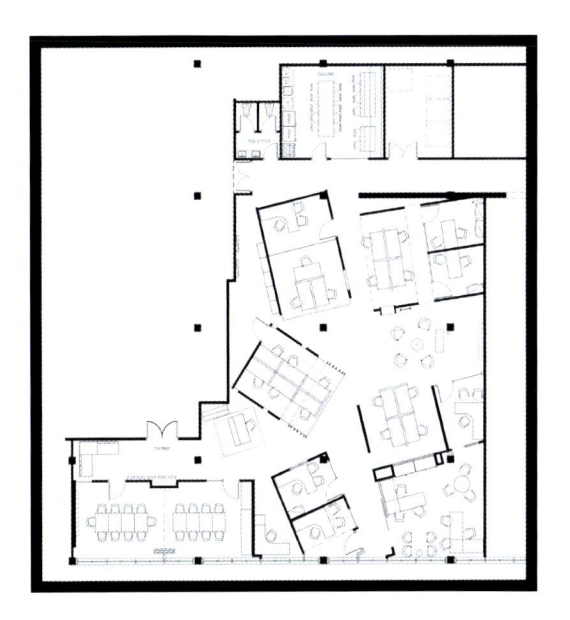

DESIGNING SPACES | Designliga

↑ | **Building paneling,** Dibond
→ | **Triton copper chair,** by Classicon

Halle A

Munich

Halle A is the studio of the Munich office of Designliga in a former locksmith's shop in the Munich municipal utility plant. The interplay between architectural atmosphere, the real world of digitalized work and a contemporary longing for intimacy and material security is the spawning ground for the design concept. The staging atmosphere of brick walls, exposed crane ways and floor surfaces with end grain parquet flooring made of larch was retained. The most striking architectural intervention is the pair of double decker saddle-back roofs which structure the hall. They individually define spaces and draw attention to the outer area, without creating hard boundaries.

PROJECT FACTS **Location:** Hans-Preißinger-Straße 8, Halle A, 81379 Munich, Germany. **Client:** Designliga, Form & Code. **Completion:** 2012. **Gross floor area:** 640 m². **Type of business:** design studio.

DESIGNING SPACES   DESIGNLIGA

↑ | **Desks,** custom-designed
← | **SWM industrial complex**
↓ | **Floor plan**
↗ | **Saddleback roofed houses,** structure the space
→ | **Co-workers' kitchen,** as private area

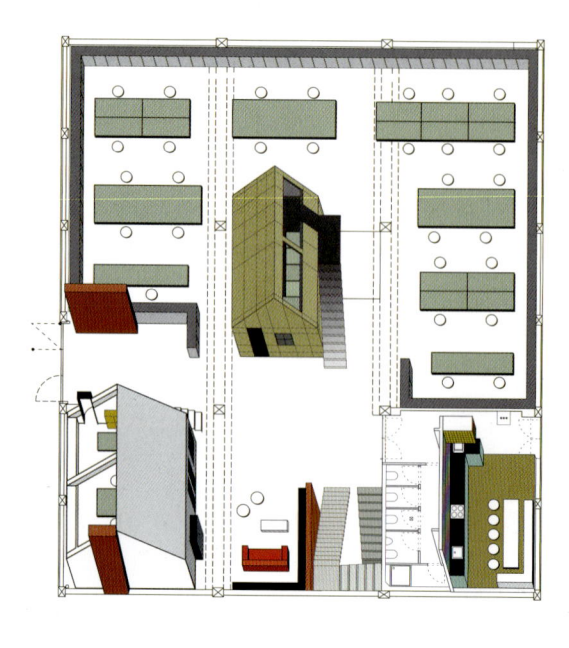

HALLE A

DESIGNING SPACES | Fraher Architects

↑ | **Exterior view**
→ | **Interior view**, office

The Green Studio

London

Sited opposite the Butterfly House, The Green Studio is a garden based creative home workspace for an architectural practice. The design for the building in the south-east of London was driven by the director's need to balance the demands of a young family with an increasing workload. The studio's shape and orientation was the result of a detailed sunlight analysis minimizing its impact on the surrounding buildings and ensuring high levels of day light in the garden and workspaces. The split levels and grounded form helps to conceal its mass and facilitates the transition between the garden and studio. Clad in a stainless steel mesh the terraced planter beds and wild flower green roofs will combine to green the façade and replace the lost habitat.

PROJECT FACTS **Location:** London, United Kingdom. **Architect and contractor:** Fraher Architects. **Completion:** 2013. **Gross floor area:** 32 m². **Type of business:** architecture studio.

DESIGNING SPACES   FRAHER ARCHITECTS

THE GREEN STUDIO

←← | Workspace with staircase
↑ | Interior view
← | Rooftop
↓ | Floor plan

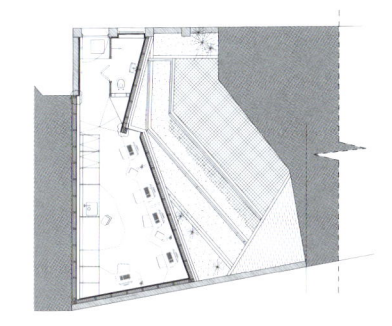

DESIGNING SPACES | Stephen Williams Associates

↑ | Kitchen
→ | Hallway

Jung von Matt Headquarters

Hamburg

In 2010, the agency group Jung von Matt commissioned Stephen Williams Associates to extend one of their offices in Hamburg's trendy "Karolinenviertel" by two floors to accommodate the management and the accounting departments. The 19th century factory building is almost occupied by Jung von Matt. The management now resides on the fourth floor in a space that was quickly dubbed the "elephant house". In the staff cafe, one feels like being on the inside of the Trojan horse, the agency's role model. It is an entirely wood-clad, comfortable space for informal conversation over tea or coffee, which so often creates the spark for big ideas. In close contact with Jung von Matt's management, Stephen Williams Associates has succeeded in finding a timeless design that reflects the agency's character and idiosyncrasies in every detail.

PROJECT FACTS **Location:** Glashüttenstraße, Hamburg, Germany. **Client:** Jung von Matt, advertising agency. **Completion:** 2011. **Gross floor area:** 1,600 m². **Type of business:** advertising agency.

DESIGNING SPACES STEPHEN WILLIAMS ASSOCIATES

JUNG VON MATT HEADQUARTERS

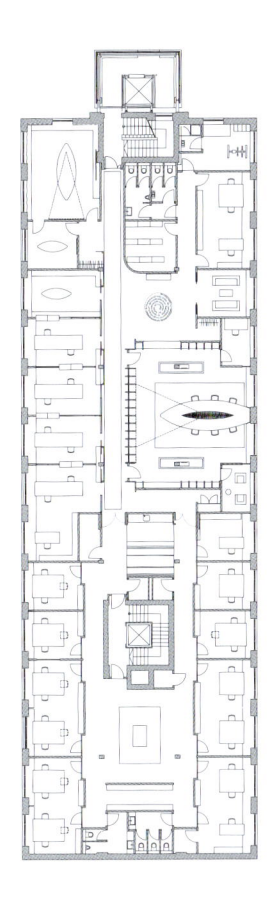

←← | **First floor,** the trojan horse track
← | **Office**
↑ | **Plan**
↓ | **Hallway**

DESIGNING SPACES | Eriksen Skajaa Architects

↑ | **Meeting room**
→ | **Lunch room**, with grand piano

The Workshop Behind The Scenes

Bergen

The festival offices were formerly located in an old bank building with large individual offices. The design of the new premises included open plan offices for the festival's mainly project-based work and spaces with a high degree of flexibility. The use of the space changes during the year, from a planning phase to the festival period, when the activity and number of employees increases. It requires several workspaces of different sizes, both to accommodate the workforce and to effectively use the space. The festival offices are imagined as workshops where the festivals are made, but also as the activity behind the scenes of what's happening on stage.

| PROJECT FACTS | **Location:** Torggaten 5, Bergen, Norway. **Client:** Bergen International Festival / Gjølanger bruk. **Completion:** 2013. **Gross floor area:** 450 m². **Type of business:** offices for culture and music festival.

DESIGNING SPACES   ERIKSEN SKAJAA ARCHITECTS

THE WORKSHOP BEHIND THE SCENES

←← | **Meeting room and lunch room**
↑ | **Wooden box,** around staircase
← | **Corridor**

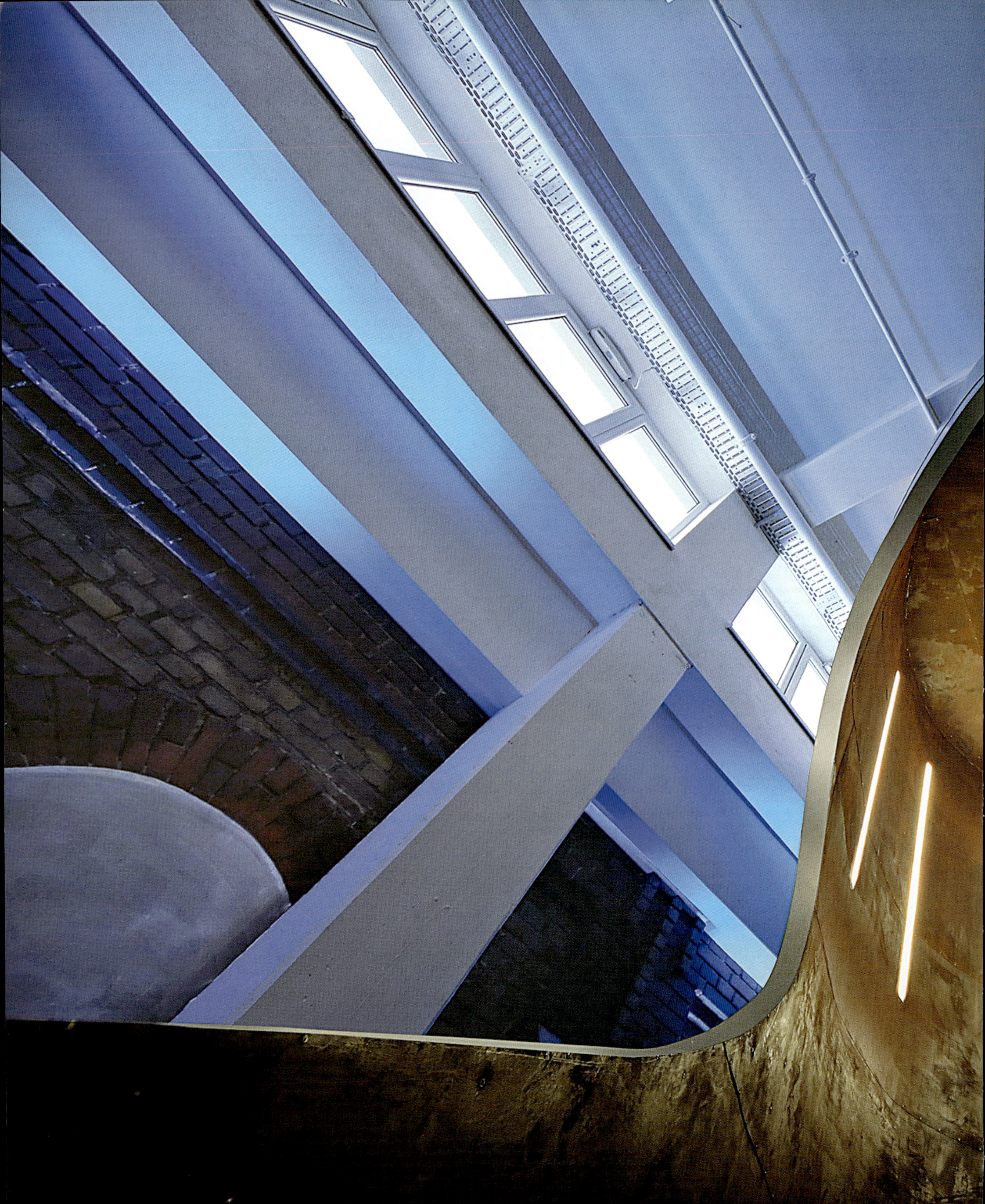

THINKING TOGETHER

| THINKING TOGETHER | KINZO Berlin |

↑ | **Exterior view**
→ | **Staircase**, connecting the entrance hall with the cafeteria

SoundCloud Headquarters

Berlin

The new headquarters for the online platform SoundCloud are located on three floors and approximately 4,000 square meters of an old brewery along the former Berlin Wall. The 180 employees of the rapidly growing start-ups meet here, which is currently the most important nodal point for the musical exchange in the internet. There is space for up to 350 people. The architectural office of KINZO was commissioned by SoundCloud to create a spatial identity for the young company and to provide an appropriate architectonic framework for the unusual work structures. The new headquarters is intended to forge new paths as a place for creativity and innovation in the Berlin office landscape and to both shape and accompany the company on their way in the coming years.

PROJECT FACTS **Location:** Rheinsberger Straße 76/77, 10115 Berlin, Germany. **Other creatives involved:** Kelly Robinson. **Client:** SoundCloud. **Completion:** 2014. **Gross floor area:** 4,000 m². **Type of business:** music, online, streaming-platform.

THINKING TOGETHER   KINZO BERLIN

← | **Lounge area,** near the entrance
↓ | **The lights in the work areas,** a combination of light and acoustic object

SOUNDCLOUD HEADQUARTERS

← | **Conference room**, "Mission"
↑ | **Floor plan**
↓ | **Fireplace room**, "The Den"

THINKING TOGETHER | Neri&Hu Design and Research Office

↑ | Hall
→ | Open office space
↗ | Raw concrete fittings

Flamingo Shanghai Office – The Attic

Shanghai

In Gaston Bachelard's seminal work, "The Poetics of Space", he poses a metaphor of the house as a dwelling for the psyche; while the cellar represents our deep subconscious, the attic is a space of quiet and rational thought. In imaginations and memories, the attic is an oft forgotten space, a space of contradictions and possibilities, both dark and light, intimate and vast, daunting and comforting. Neri&Hu's renovation of an industrial roof space in Shanghai into offices for the leading global insight and strategic consultancy, Flamingo, are inspired by these very paradoxical and enigmatic notions of the attic.

PROJECT FACTS **Location:** 207 Mengzi Road, Building 11, 7F, Shanghai, China. **Architect:** Neri&Hu Design and Research Office. **Principals-in-charge:** Lyndon Neri, Rossana Hu. **Completion:** 2014. **Gross floor area:** 620 m². **Type of business:** strategic consultancy.

THINKING TOGETHER

NERI&HU DESIGN AND RESEARCH OFFICE

↑ | **Interior view**
← | **Lounge area**

FLAMINGO SHANGHAI OFFICE – THE ATTIC

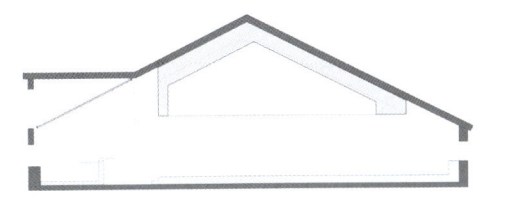

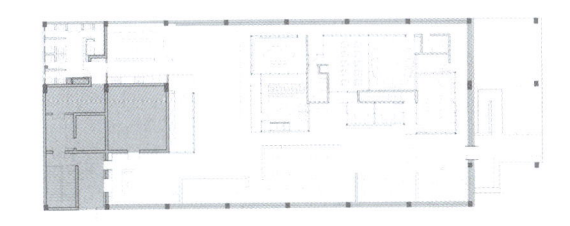

← | Conference room
↑ | Section and floor plan
↓ | Interior view

THINKING TOGETHER | SKA
Sibylle Kramer Architekten

↑ | Open workspace
→ | Central space

SKA Studio

Hamburg

The Fettstrasse industrial building was constructed around 1900 for purposes like woodworking or the manufacturing of chocolates. Today the courtyard building houses charming studio spaces. The rough character of the building guides the material concept and selection of furnishings. Studio SKA Sibylle Kramer Architekten functions in an open work atmosphere which can be rearranged at will with the same boxes. In the entryway the elements serve as a plugged-in wardrobe and reception desk while to the side of the central middle axis they define the work islands without truncating the space as a whole. The height of the boxes is oriented to the desks and allows for an unencumbered view. The walls of the central common area define a zero-line at eye level, underscoring the exhibition concept of the works on display.

PROJECT FACTS **Location:** Fettstraße 7a, 20357 Hamburg, Germany. **Client:** SKA Sibylle Kramer Architekten. **Completion:** 2011. **Gross floor area:** 168 m². **Type of business:** architecture studio.

THINKING TOGETHER SKA SIBYLLE KRAMER ARCHITEKTEN

↑ | Entrance area
← | Workspace

SKA STUDIO

89

↑ | Entrance hall
← | Floor plan

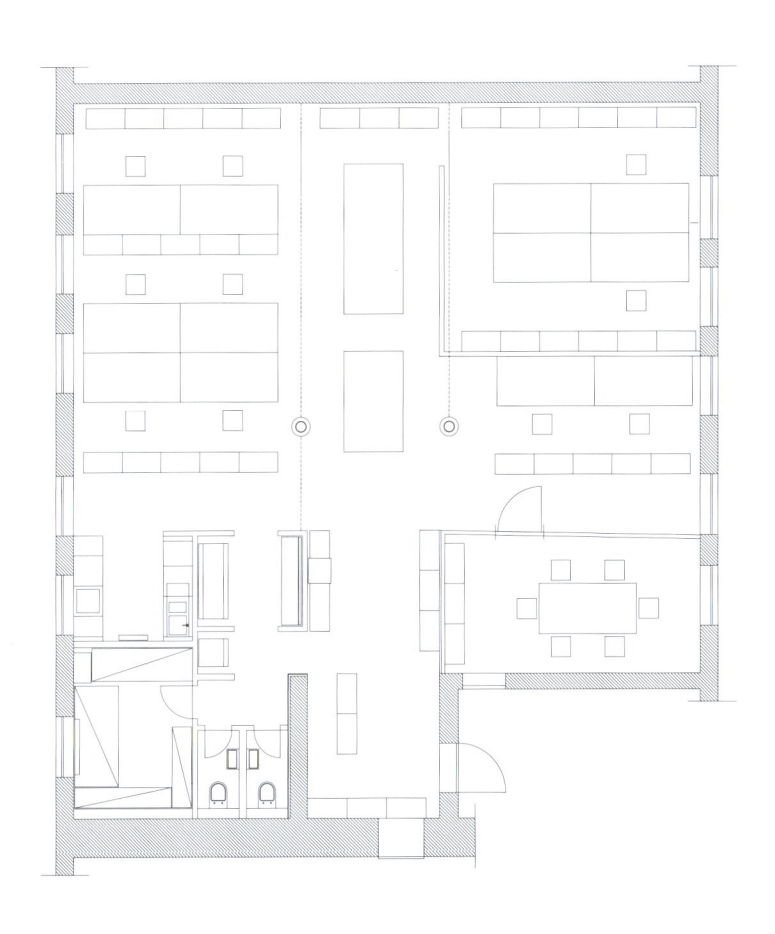

THINKING TOGETHER | Corvin Cristian

↑ | Workspace
→ | Meeting room

Headvertising Offices

Bucharest

Inside the former Romanian Stock Exchange building, the shipping crates act as furniture, storage, movable dividing walls, dynamic company statement and reverence for the genius loci. The oversized lamps and the chesterfields add a cozy feeling to the otherwise austere design. The natural texture of plywood provides warmth. Stock Exchange is the process of moving goods. An advertising agency is moving brands (which is moving goods as well), thus the moving shipping crates are a metaphor both for the company activity and for the former use of this historical building.

PROJECT FACTS **Location:** 150 Uranus Street, Bucharest, Romania. **Client:** Headvertising agency. **Completion:** 2008. **Gross floor area:** 400 m². **Type of business:** advertising agency.

THINKING TOGETHER CORVIN CRISTIAN

HEADVERTISING OFFICES

←← | **Relax area**
↑ | **Workspace**, plywood furniture
↙ | **Floor plan**

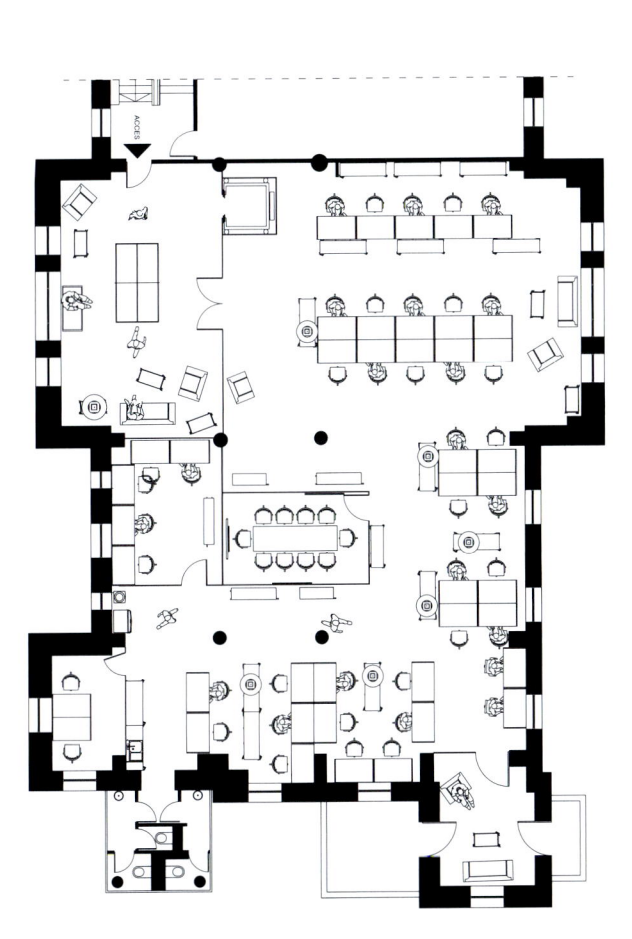

THINKING TOGETHER | Peter Sampson Architecture Studio

↑ | **Exterior view**
↗ | **View towards bikeLAB**
→ | **Interior view,** at work inside bikeLAB

UWSA bikeLAB

Winnipeg

This project asks that the term "infrastructure" which is typically used in the context of engineering and mega projects, be re-fitted to the living conditions and human context of a city. A fleet of decommissioned sea containers are planned to construct a light-infrastructure network of social nodes or hubs that enable and support the emergence of a bicycle-transit strategy in Winnipeg, Canada. Each of these hubs is planned to be comprised of two reclaimed 6-meter-long shipping containers, providing bicycle storage along with service tools and an adjacent amenity space such as an information booth or coffee shop. Designed as a kind of adaptable kit, the first of these hubs is bikeLAB, a prototype workshop that transforms two redundant containers into a highly visible and centralized community workspace operated by volunteers.

PROJECT FACTS **Location:** University of Winnipeg, Winnipeg, Canada. **Client:** University of Winnipeg students' association. **Completion:** 2011. **Gross floor area:** 32.5 m². **Type of business:** cycling workshop.

95

THINKING TOGETHER

PETER SAMPSON ARCHITECTURE STUDIO

↑ | Interior view
↓ | Section

UWSA BIKELAB

↑ | **View,** towards entrance
← | **Detail of container,** door with signage
↓ | **Floor plan**

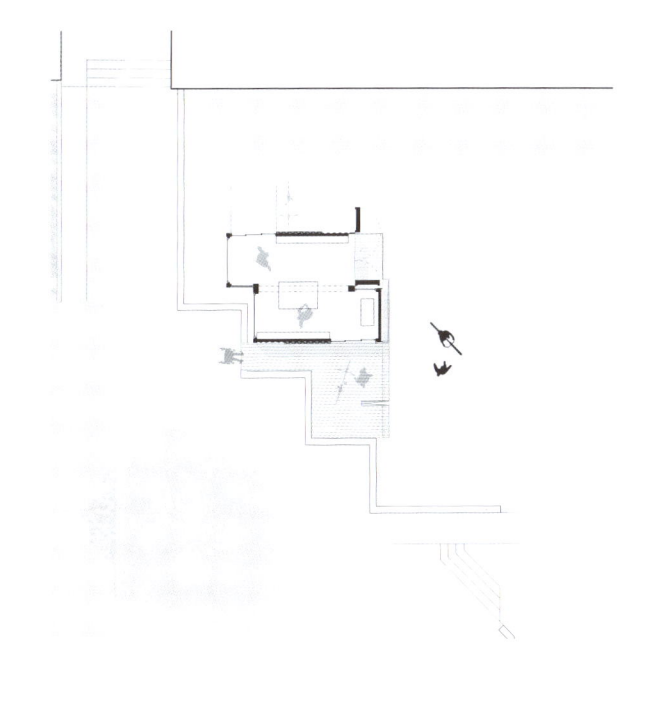

THINKING TOGETHER | Peter Stasek Architects – Corporate Architecture

↑ | **Tower stairwell**, illuminated brick wall
↗ | **Open space office**
→ | **Tower stairwell**

Ajando Next Level CRM

Mannheim

The core business of "ajando.CRM" is the acquisition, processing and transmission of information. The dynamic of these flows can be seen as a vector for the whole company. In making visible this dynamic of the flows of information, architect Peter Stasek not only considers them as a creative approach for the redesign of the space. They are in fact the basis for the new Ajando corporate architecture concept. The spatial arrangement of the functional area as well as their access in the Loft-Office-Concept of Ajando is shaped according to the motto of the famous Viennese architect from the turn of the 19th century, Josef M. Hoffmann: "The path's goal is also the goal of the space".

PROJECT FACTS **Location:** Industriestraße 35, 68169 Mannheim, Germany. **Other creatives involved:** Luana Kroner-Stasek, Licht-Team Speyer, Loftwerk. **Client:** Ajando GmbH. **Completion:** 2013. **Gross floor area:** 750 m². **Type of business:** cross media agency.

THINKING TOGETHER   PETER STASEK ARCHITECTS – CORPORATE ARCHITECTURE

↑ | Tower stairwell and open space office
← | Floor plans

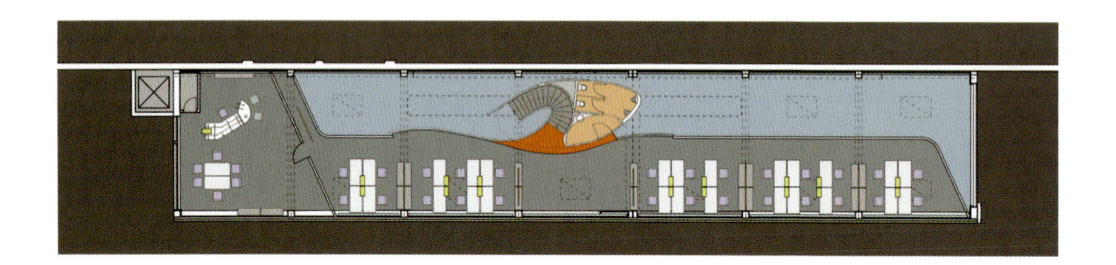

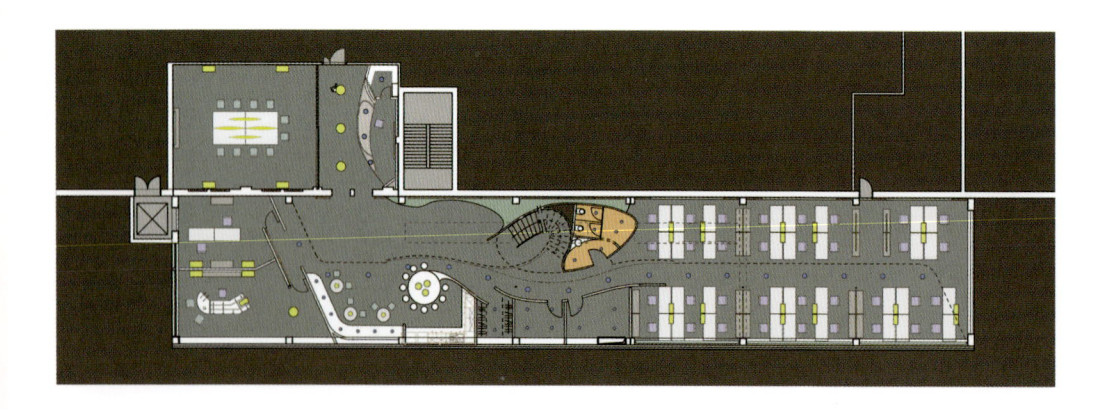

AJANDO NEXT LEVEL CRM

↑ | Lounge and tower stairwell
← | Detail of the stairwell

THINKING TOGETHER | Holst Architecture

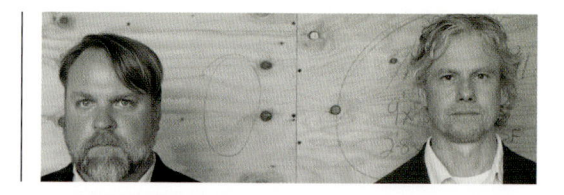

↑ | Laser-cut birch plywood wraps
↓ | Light-filled flexible gallery space

↙ | Gallery
↓ | Gallery and kitchen
→ | Interior view

Panic, Inc.

Portland

The Panic, Inc. headquarters project is a renovation and interior architectural design of an existing wood-framed warehouse in Portland, Oregon. The studio provides the local software design firm with a workspace that reflects its creativity while providing a home away from home for employees who spend long days at the office. The overall goal was to create a design that was fun but not zany, restrained but not austere. The office is a culmination of two spaces: a light-filled flexible gallery space, and an open workspace with controlled lighting and views to the north and east. A variety of finishes, colors, patterns, and textures provide a playful sophistication and subtle reference to Panic's corporate alter ego. Colorful graphic panels, carpet patterns, and playful art on the walls reinforce the vibrant, creative atmosphere of the space.

PROJECT FACTS **Location:** 315 SW 11th Ave. 400, Portland, OR 97205, USA. **Interior design consultant:** Osmose Design. **Completion:** 2008. **Gross floor area:** 662 m². **Type of business:** software design.

THINKING TOGETHER   HOLST ARCHITECTURE

↑ | **Open office**
← | **Lounge space,** for staff and clients with custom textiles
↓ | **Floor plan**

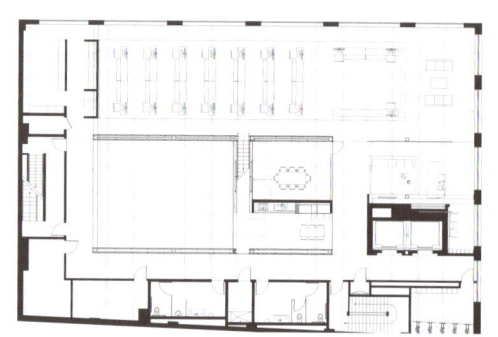

PANIC, INC.

← | **Interior view,** the studio
↓ | **Lounge,** with view of the founders room at left

THINKING TOGETHER | Studio O+A

↑ | **Reception,** with custom ceiling
↗ | **Coffee bar,** music room and lounge
→ | **Yurts**

Cisco

San Francisco

The view of San Francisco's waterfront from Cisco's new offices in some ways sets the theme for O+A's design. At the outset O+A surveyed the company's employees to find out what they liked about their old, much smaller headquarters. A consensus emerged for natural light and plenty of collaboration space. The size of the new office and the prominence of its floor-to-ceiling windows made collaboration and natural light relatively easy bills to fill. O+A's design offers a variety of formal and informal, indoor and outdoor meeting spaces. The scale and the light support both a rich palette of colors and design elements tailored to the broad canvas.

PROJECT FACTS **Location:** San Francisco, CA, USA. **Client:** Cisco. **Completion:** 2013. **Gross floor area:** 10,219 m². **Type of business:** technology company.

THINKING TOGETHER　　　　STUDIO O+A

CISCO 109

←← | **Lounge area**, with hanging tillandsia
↑ | **Sliding doors**, to lounge area
← | **Floor plan**

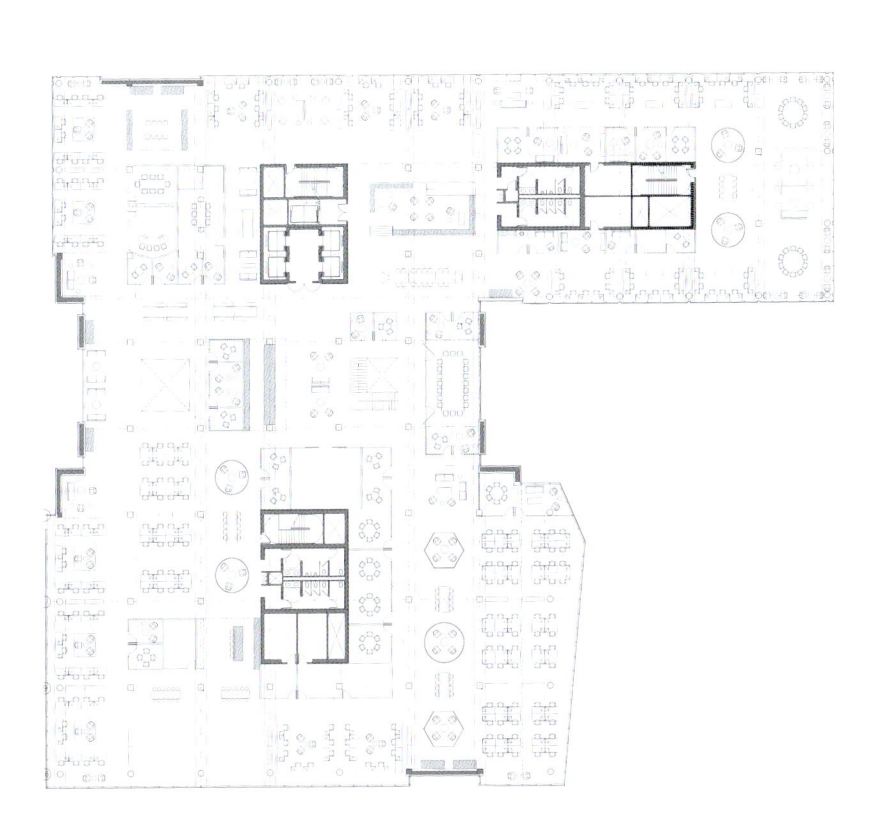

THINKING TOGETHER | Studioninedots

↑ | **Staircase**
→ | **General view**, lobby

De Burgemeester

Hoofddorp

The office building on the Burgemeester Pabstlaan dates back to the 1970s and is centrally located in Hoofddorp close to Amsterdam. The task was to respond to the current market by increasing the number of rentable spaces and making the building more flexible. At the same time a strong identity that contributes to better recognition, communication and functioning for the new companies is created: We Space. That's the name for the communal area at the heart of the building. It's a place that brings people together. By enlarging the existing void and connecting the floors to a spectacular staircase, new physical connections were established. The staircase as a vehicle for communication lends the building a collective identity and a social space where people can meet. As a vertical lobby that offers views of all floors, it tells occupants that they are part of a larger world.

PROJECT FACTS **Location:** Burgemeester Pabstlaan, Hoofddorp, The Netherlands. **Client:** Ymere | Lingotto. **Completion:** 2013. **Total area:** 980 m². **Type of business:** commercial company.

THINKING TOGETHER   STUDIONINEDOTS

↑ | Kitchen
← | Office space
↓ | Floor plan

DE BURGEMEESTER

← | Staircase
↑ | Isometry
↓ | Offices

THINKING TOGETHER

Simon Bush-King
Architecture & Urbanism

↑ | **Central atrium and conference room**
↗ | **Meeting rooms,** located in each of the large studios corners
→ | **Interior view,** meeting room

Superheroes

Amsterdam

Simon Bush-King's clients, digital agency Superheroes required room for new sidekicks and their expanding cape collection, finding a fantastic light-filled space in central Amsterdam. However a short lease of only three years dictated a budget which was only a quarter that of a 'normal' low budget for fit-out work. The architects took a targeted approach that developed their clients wishes, visual expression and construction methods in unison. Accepting corners create character the team located much needed meeting rooms in each corner of the large open space with flexible spaces introduced in-between for the myriad of tasks that defy description in studio environments, the casual chat, quick review or private phone call. The studio adopts a simple, clean expression using elements of Superheroes own identity.

PROJECT FACTS **Location:** Amsterdam, The Netherlands. **Design team:** Joti Weijers-Coghlan, Sarah Rowlands. **Client:** Superheroes. **Completion:** 2014. **Gross floor area:** 480 m². **Type of business:** digital agency.

THINKING TOGETHER   SIMON BUSH-KING ARCHITECTURE & URBANISM

SUPERHEROES

←← | Reception
↑ | **Moveable furniture,** divides the studio
← | **Interior of a project room**
↓ | **Floor plan**

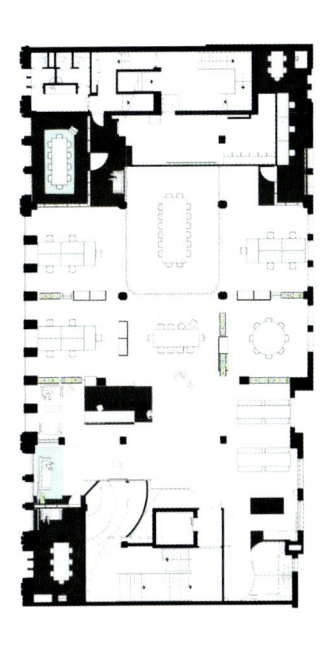

THINKING TOGETHER | Particular

↑ | Office workspace
→ | Library discussion table

Particular Studio

Melbourne

Located in the heart of Melbourne, this small studio space is designed for architecture practice. A particular concern has been to create a space of many faces. The idea was a studio that allowed the co-workers to take on multiple characters, a space to be big or small in, while roving from solo, to team, to crowd. This had to be an arrangement which could be broken down without losing the sense of generosity and openness. It also had to be embedded with opportunity, an infrastructure for work, creating and making. The design of the studio space was brought about by a combination of necessity and a flexible space which could support different roles for the users at different times.

PROJECT FACTS **Location:** Little Collins Street 365, Melbourne, Australia. **Client:** Particular. **Completion:** 2014. **Gross floor area:** 60 m². **Type of business:** architectural design.

THINKING TOGETHER   PARTICULAR

← | **Communal work bench**
↓ | **"Plug and play"**, table surfaces

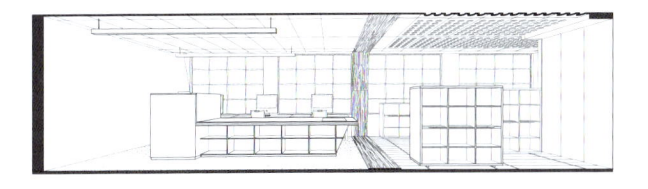

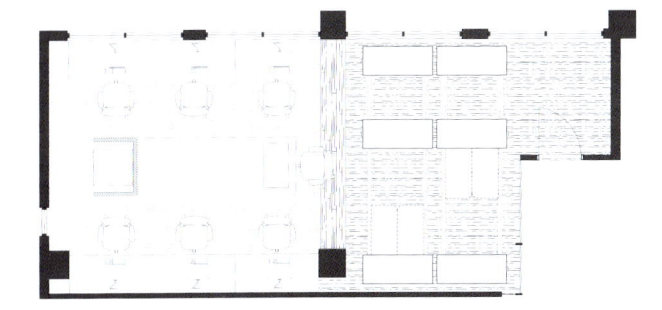

PARTICULAR STUDIO

← | Workspace vs. the transformer
↑ | Sectional perspective and floor plan
↓ | Freedom of configuration

THINKING TOGETHER | Design Blitz

↑ | **Showroom and mezzanine**
↗ | **Custom steel screen graphic**, at exterior
→ | **Garage door**, indoor to exterior

One Workplace Showroom and Headquarters

Santa Clara

For its new headquarters and showroom, One Workplace wanted to create a bleeding-edge, world class workplace. Design Blitz collaborated with the company to combine an existing stand-alone, mid-century office building with a neighboring warehouse to create 35,000 square feet of office, showroom, and workspace. The most prominent element of the interior is the mezzanine structure, which the architects designed as a configuration of two "c"-shaped structures stacked at an angle to each other. This structure serves multiple functions, housing an elevated conference room and also serving as an observation platform that allows members of the One Workplace team to quickly survey the floor and show customers each product in action.

PROJECT FACTS **Location:** Santa Clara, CA, USA. **General contractor:** OPI Builders. **Client:** One Workplace. **Completion:** 2013. **Gross floor area:** 3,250 m². **Type of business:** furniture dealer.

THINKING TOGETHER   DESIGN BLITZ

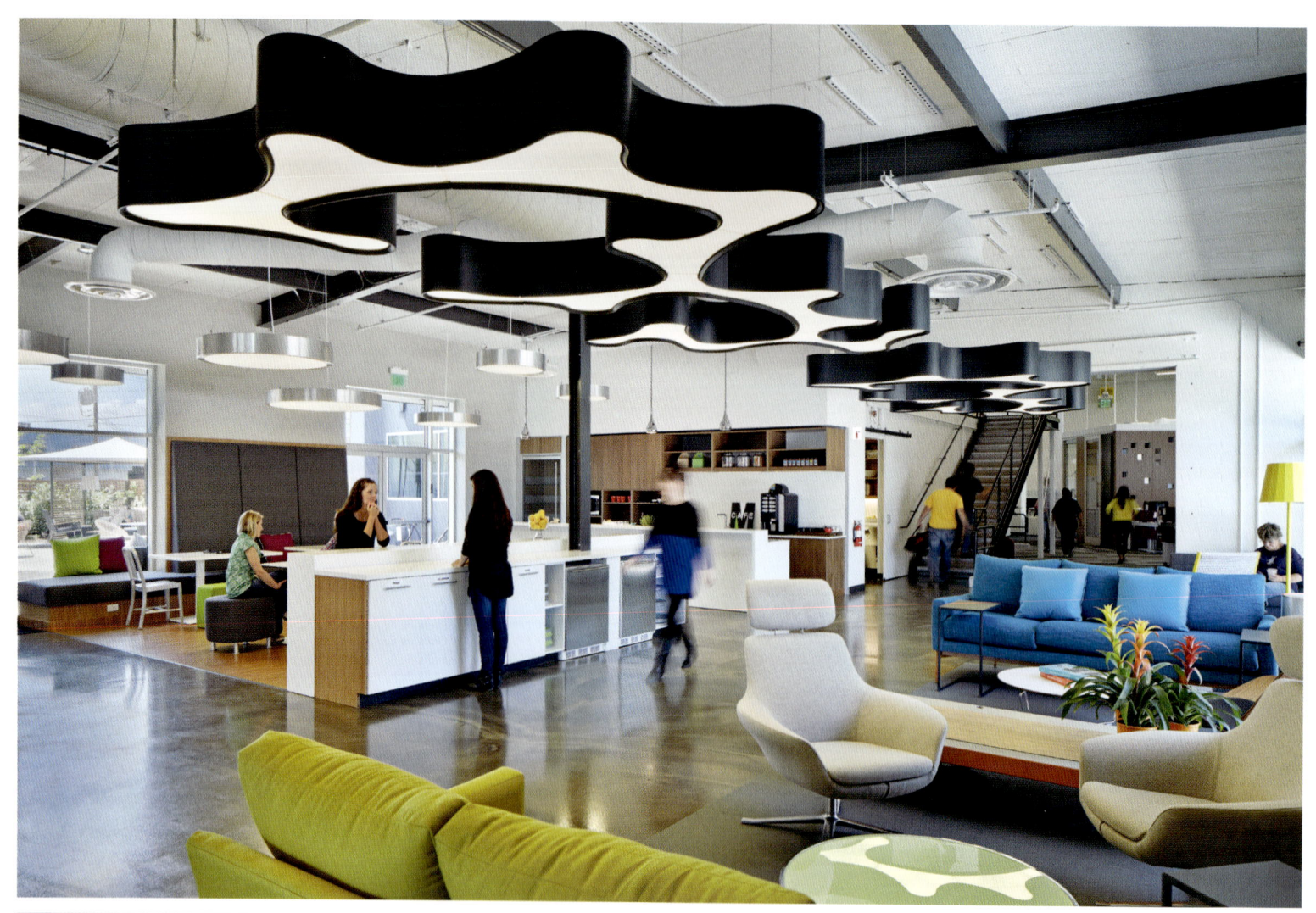

↑ | **General view,** the work cafe
← | **The work cafe**

ONE WORKPLACE SHOWROOM AND HEADQUARTERS

↑ | View of the mezzanine
← | Showroom and workspace
↓ | Axonometric view

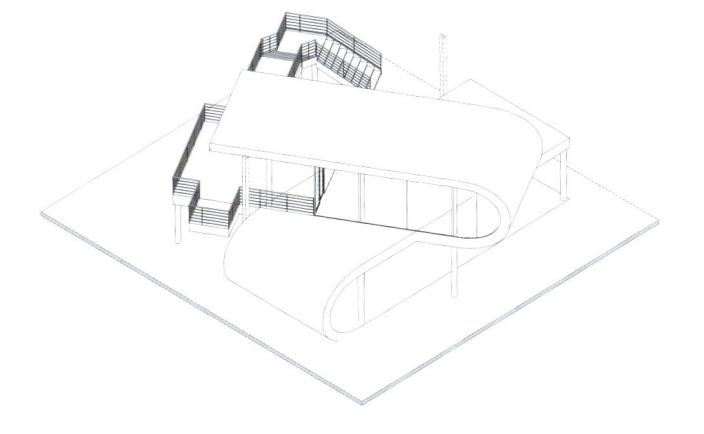

THINKING TOGETHER | Petokraka

↑ | **Entrance to upper floor,** park lamp
↗ | **Workshop,** kitchen and lounge in the back
→ | **Conference room**

Nova Iskra Design Incubator

Belgrade

The first design incubator in the region of South-East Europe, Nova Iskra, opened its doors in Belgrade. It is a co-working space dedicated to the professionalization of designers in Serbia and the region, and to establishing connections between the creative industries and manufacturing. The multi-functional workspace was established to support young creatives from the fields of design, architecture, interior design, visual communications and related fields. A rundown office space of 350 square meters in Gavrila Principa Street in downtown Belgrade has been fully renovated by the Belgrade-based architecture studio Petokraka. Lightness, simplicity and attention to detail are the main characteristics of the overall articulation of space.

| PROJECT FACTS | **Location:** Gavrila Principa 43, Belgrade, Serbia. **Client:** Nova Iskra Design Incubator. **Completion:** 2012. **Gross floor area:** 350 m². **Type of business:** co-working.

THINKING TOGETHER   PETOKRAKA

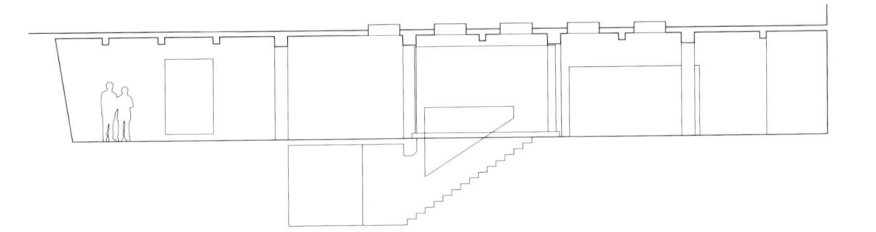

NOVA ISKRA DESIGN INCUBATOR

←← | **Entrance to upper floor**, park lamp
↑ | **Co-working space**
← | **Floor plans and section**

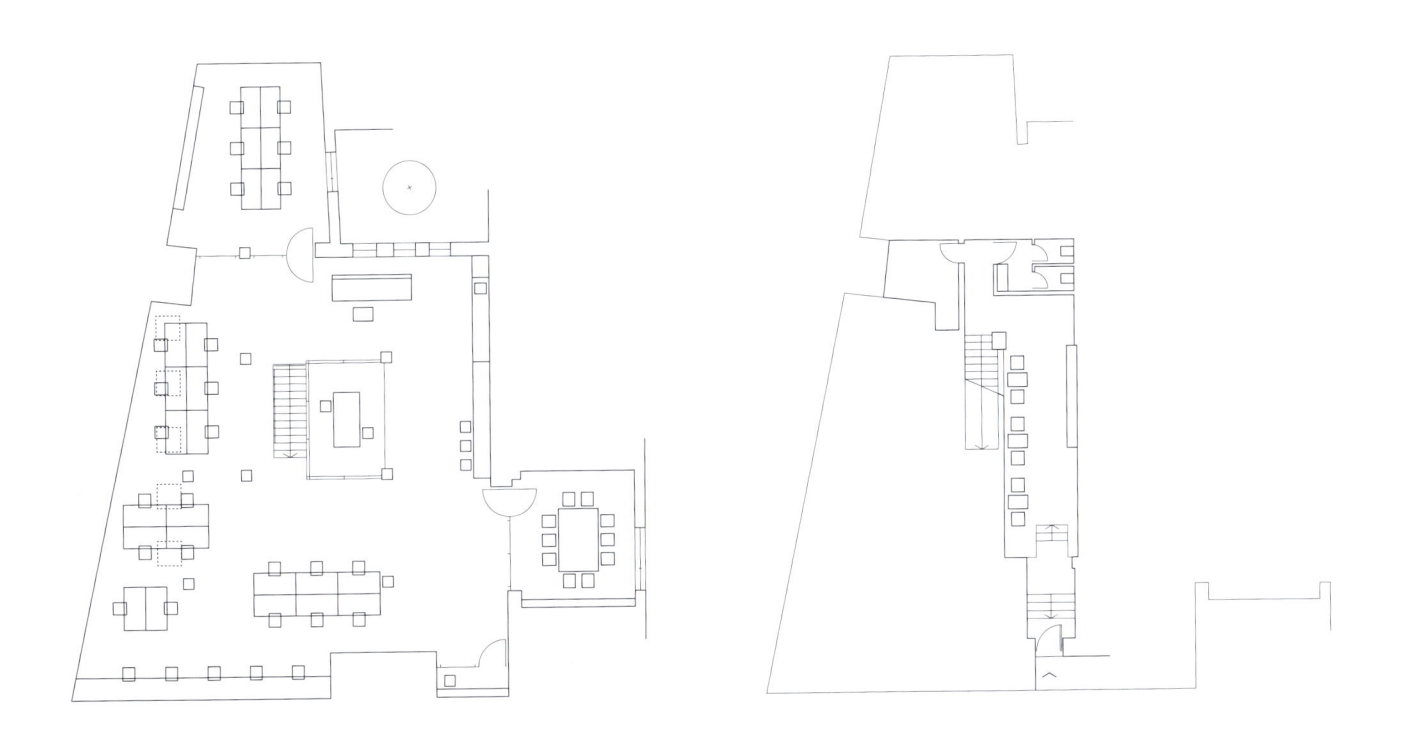

THINKING TOGETHER

Ector Hoogstad Architecten

↑ | **Main view,** hall
→ | **View from staircase**

Kantoor IMD

Rotterdam

The design strategy positioned all work areas on two floors in air-conditioned zones against the closed end walls. From there, they overlook the hall, in which pavilions with conference areas were created, interlinked by footbridges and various types of stairs. An unusual layout for an office building, it allows users to be in constant contact with its spatial and social heart, stimulating interaction. The hall itself was designed as a weakly air-conditioned cavity, which lends itself very well to many uses, including informal consultations, lectures, exhibitions and lunching. Large new windows in what was originally a closed façade, in combination with the existing skylights in the roof, provide daylight and magnificent panoramic views of the water.

PROJECT FACTS **Location:** 77 Piekstraat, Rotterdam, The Netherlands. **Furniture design:** Ector Hoogstad Architects. **Client:** IMd raadgevende ingenieurs. **Completion:** 2011. **Total area:** 2,014 m². **Type of business:** engineering company.

THINKING TOGETHER ECTOR HOOGSTAD ARCHITECTEN

↑ | Workspace
← | Entrance

KANTOOR IMD

↑ | Staircase
← | Central space
↓ | Sections

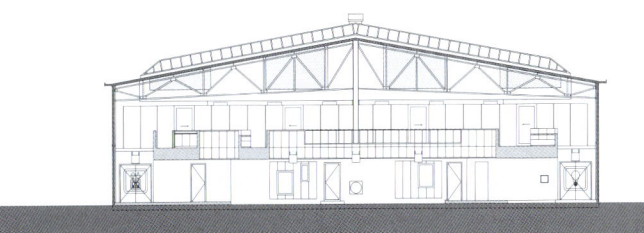

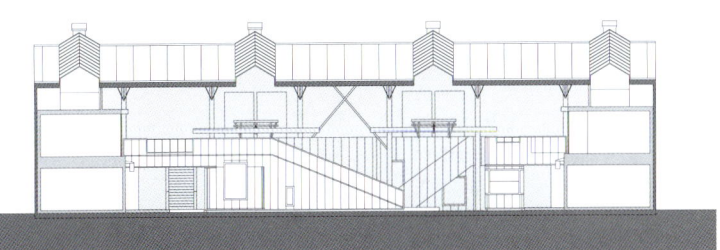

THINKING TOGETHER

Hadi Teherani AG
Hadi Teherani Interior GmbH

↑ | **Studio with view of HafenCity**

HOME4 Designstudio

Hamburg

New dimensions for work were created in the Hadi Teherani AG studio in Hamburg's HafenCity: rooms and furniture, levels and surfaces flow into each other and are multi-functional. The all-white studio is as inspiring as a location for the development of ideas as it is for encounters. A long table becomes a platform for communicative exchange. During the day it serves as an open workplace, and for evening events it is run up as a counter. The adjacent showroom opens the studio spaces in the Hadi Teherani designed building to the outside. Architecture and interiors merge. "Clear lines, restrained colors, perfect functionality and practical details are the hallmarks of the overall architectural and design concept".

| **PROJECT FACTS** **Location:** Am Kaiserkai 26, 20457 Hamburg, Germany. **Interior design:** Hadi Teherani. **Completion:** 2009. **Gross floor area:** 270 m². **Type of business:** design & interior design.

↑ | **Shades of white,** aluminum and endless transparence

↑ | **Expansive entrance**
↓ | **Spontaneous insights** and suggestions for the internal discussion

THINKING TOGETHER   HADI TEHERANI AG / HADI TEHERANI INTERIOR GMBH

HOME4 DESIGNSTUDIO

←← | Spatial layering
↑ | Short paths between the departments
← | Gallery
↓ | Section and floor plan

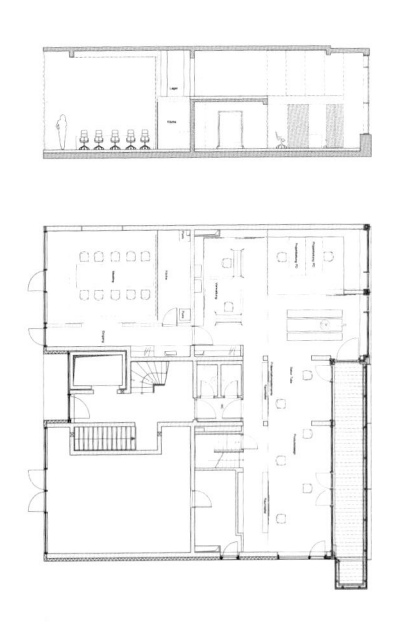

MEETING PEOPLE

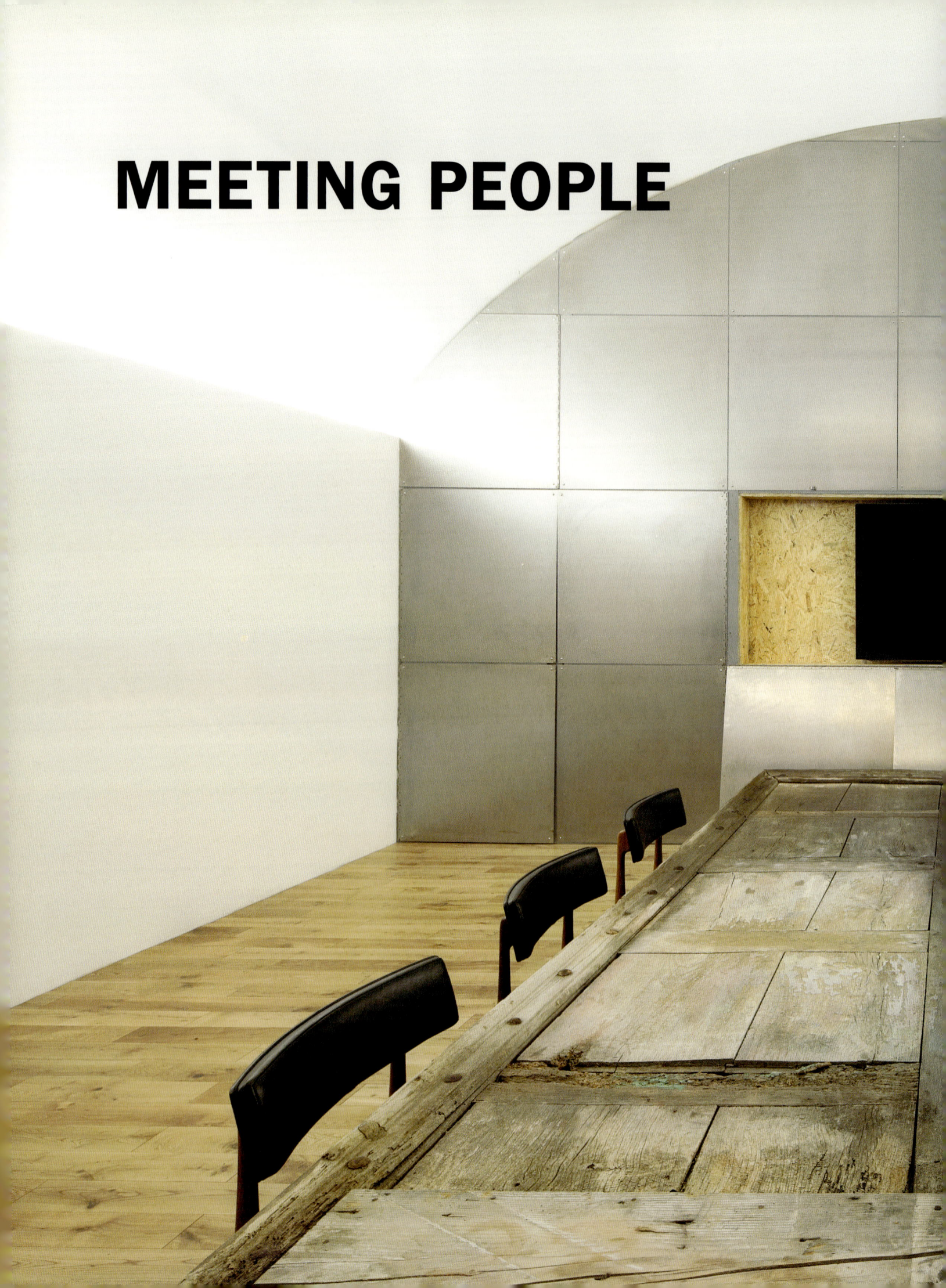

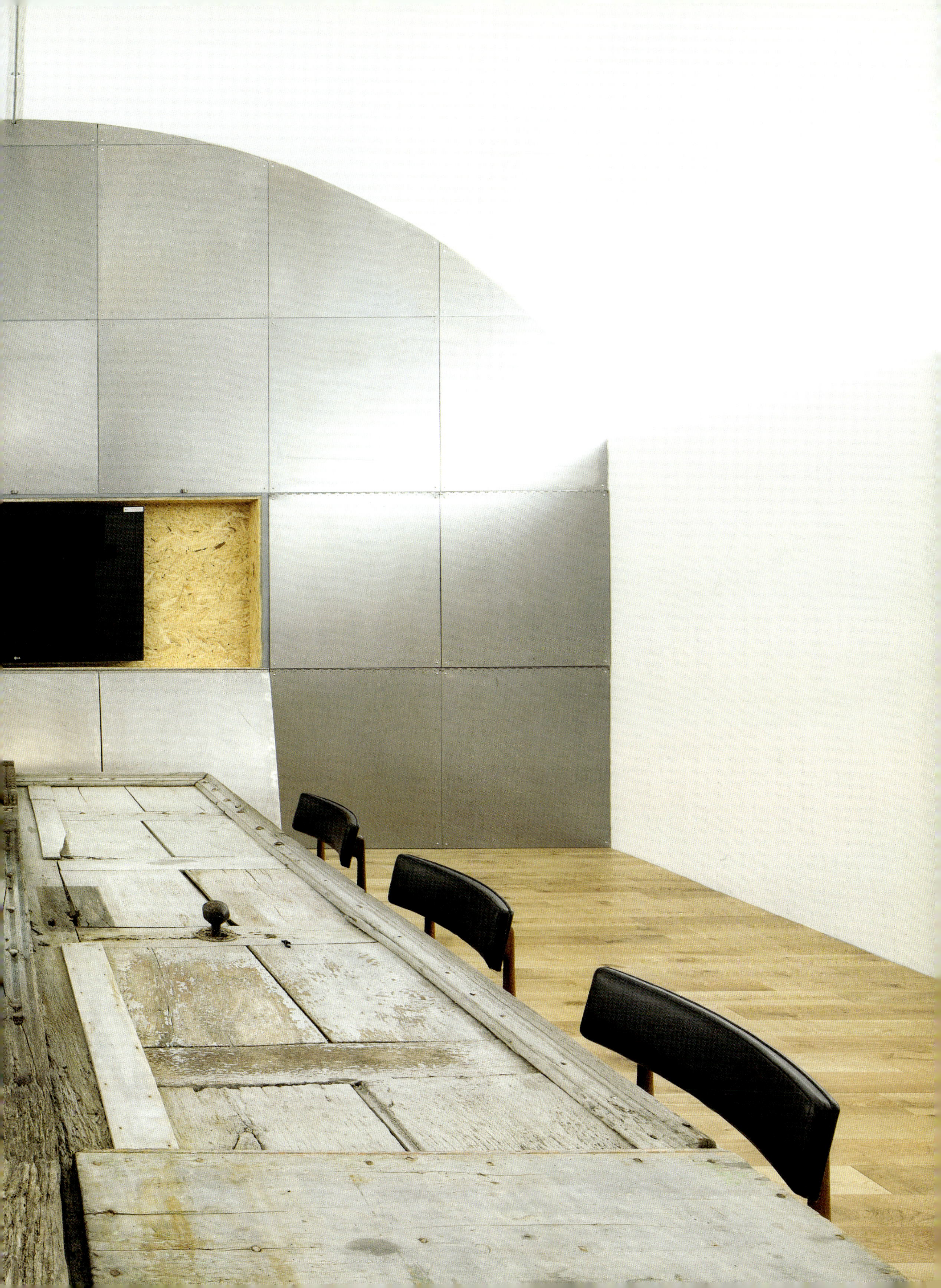

MEETING PEOPLE | Those Architects

↑ | Process room
↗ | Workstations and gym
→ | Swings and boardroom

Ansarada Office

Sydney

Collaborating closely with the clients branding agency Those Architects have turned the clients brief on its head, creating a sleek, tactile and light-filled 800 square meters space in the landmark heritage listed Metcalfe bond store, on Sydney's lower George Street, built between 1912 and 1916. The sophisticated design of the new workspace is under pinned by highly evolved technology systems that overcome the many challenges of designing for a heritage protected building.

PROJECT FACTS **Location:** George Street, Sydney, Australia. **Client:** Ansarada. **Completion:** 2013. **Gross floor area:** 800 m². **Type of business:** technology company.

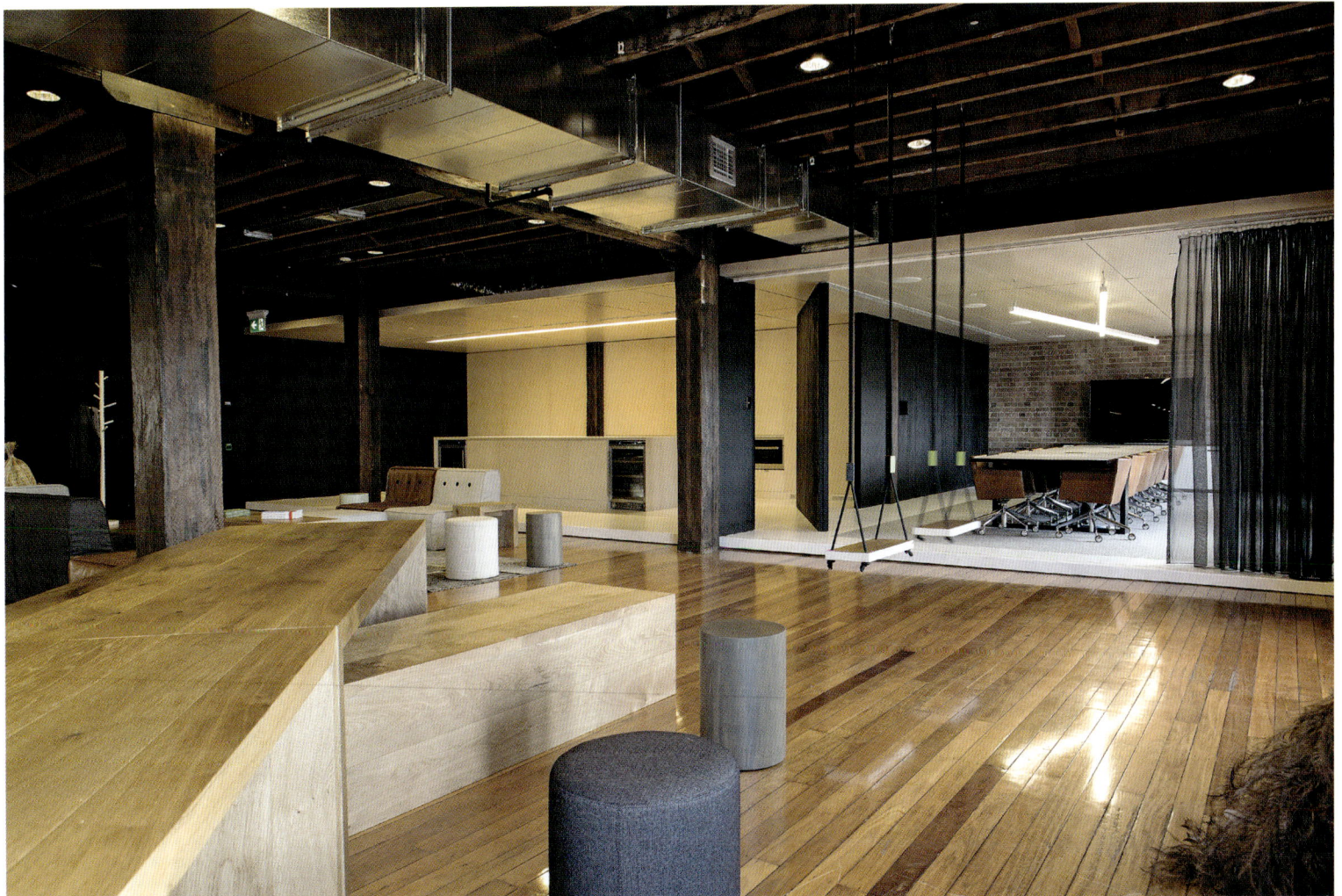

MEETING PEOPLE THOSE ARCHITECTS

↑ | Kitchen joinery
← | Recreation zone
↓ | Floor plan

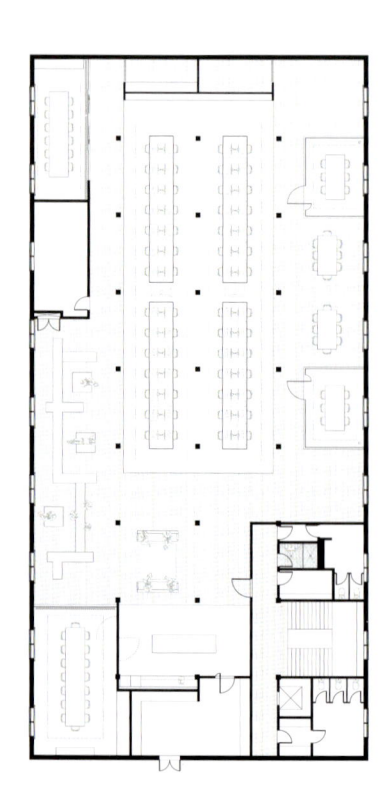

ANSARADA OFFICE

↑ | **Pegboard,** acoustic panel
← | **Workstations zone**

MEETING PEOPLE | Boora Architects

↑ | **Sales barn**
→ | **Kitchen**

FINE Design Group

Portland

This new work environment for FINE Design Group embodies the creative agency's energy and collaborative nature. Capitalizing on the exposed steel structure of the 5,475 square foot raw shell spaces, concrete floors, bood an abundance of natural light, the design team created a relaxed and loft-like open office. Nearly a quarter of the walls in the space are writeable, allowing creativity and collaboration to happen anywhere. Key elements define distinct zones. The "Barn" is a 3-pronged room that floats at the west end of the space and houses two offices and the agency's conference room. The residential-scale kitchen is a staff gathering spot and the hub for the many events the group hosts. At the east end of the office, the architect designed a walnut-clad bookcase housing an eclectic mix of books and objects.

PROJECT FACTS **Location:** Portland, Oregon, USA. **Client:** FINE Design Group. **Completion:** 2012. **Gross floor area:** 509 m². **Type of business:** creative agency.

MEETING PEOPLE — BOORA ARCHITECTS

↑ | Lounge
← | Open office
↓ | Floor plan

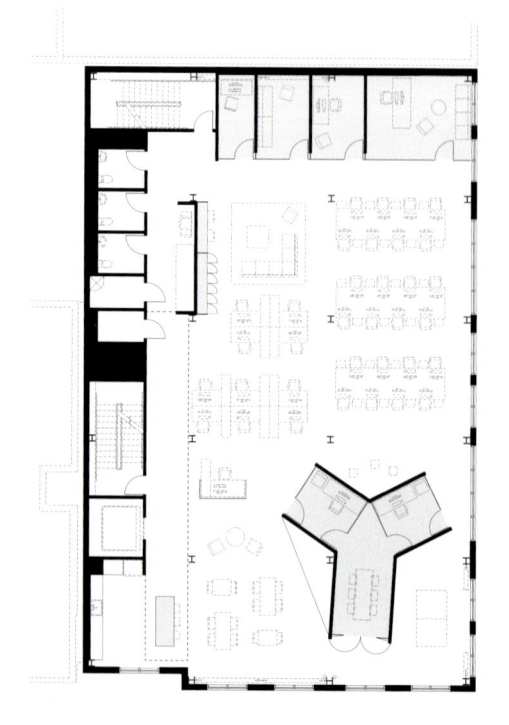

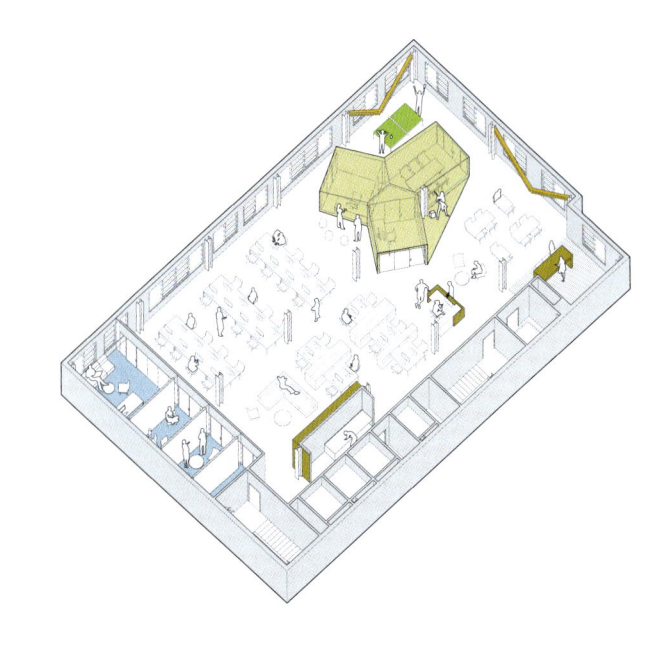

FINE DESIGN GROUP

← | Library
↑ | Axonometric view
↓ | Pool room

MEETING PEOPLE | DOS Architects

↑ | Lounge area
→ | Exterior view

MAD Office

London

DOS architects' latest creation is a stunning design for the start-up creative agency MAD London, headed by Jefferson Hack, founder of Dazed & Confused magazine. DOS' intervention was to design the top two floors of this industrial building in the ever trendy area of Old Street. The intention was to preserve the industrial character of the existing building, whilst adding a layer of warmth and modernity in the bespoke joinery and finishes and lighting. All inbuilt furnishings were designed by DOS according to the agency's clear brief of creating a distinctive and original feel for the office space. This play of light and dark, old and new is what once again distinguishes this project as another remarkable refurbishment by the DOS team.

PROJECT FACTS **Location:** London, United Kingdom. **Client:** MAD agency. **Completion:** 2012. **Gross floor area:** 240 m². **Type of business:** creative consultancy.

MEETING PEOPLE DOS ARCHITECTS

↑ | **Open office**
← | **Lounge area**

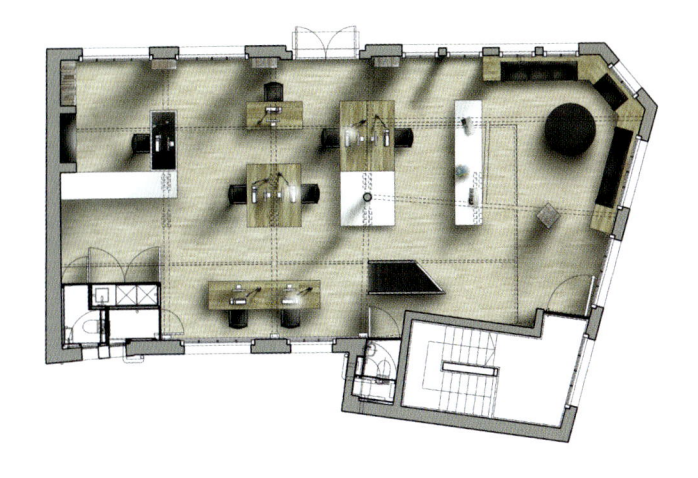

MAD OFFICE

← | Staircase
↑ | Plan
↓ | Inbuilt furnishings

MEETING PEOPLE | PL.ARCHITEKCI

↑ | **Office**
→ | **Stairs**

Workshop in the Attic

Poznan

The architects designed their own studio within a formerly disused attic space in an historic quarter of Poznan. They sought to maximize the space and reveal its character to provide an inspirational working environment whilst allowing clients to experience their style of architecture and design. The original wooden attics rafters have been expressed by creating a physical separation between them and new divisions within the space. This separation is emphasized by introducing flush white walls, cabinetry and office furniture creating a clear contrast between the old and new. 17 new windows were installed to provide the previously dark attic with natural light and a view of the neighborhood beyond the rooftops. Nothing in this office pretends to be something else; what is visible is either the architects' work or the building's original construction.

PROJECT FACTS **Location:** Ul. Dlugosza 13/12, Poznan, Poland. **Client:** PL.ARCHITEKCI. **Completion:** 2013. **Gross floor area:** 60 m². **Type of business:** architecture studio.

MEETING PEOPLE   PL.ARCHITEKCI

↑ | **First floor**
← | **Conference area**

WORKSHOP IN THE ATTIC

↑ | Hallway
← | Office
↓ | Floor plan

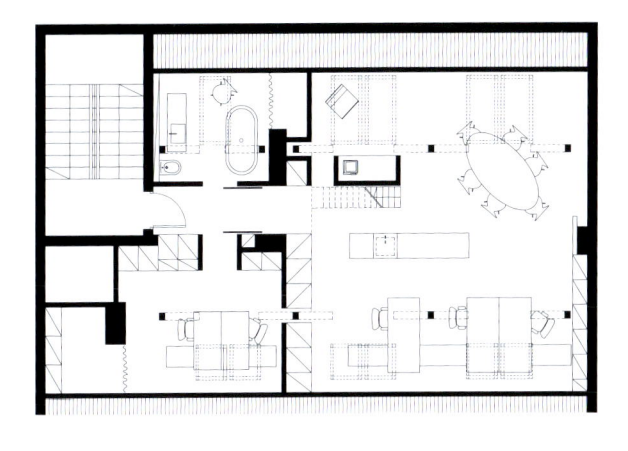

MEETING PEOPLE | sbp – Seel Bobsin Partner

↑ | Covus bar
↗ | Meeting room
→ | Corridor

Covus

Berlin

The newly renovated Covus office is located in a typical factory loft from 1898. The traditional printing publisher, Gutenberg, was formerly housed there. The high-quality, reconstructed art-nouveau façade forms the entrance to the factory area that brings to life the Berlin industrial history. These theme designed rooms offer plenty of space for formal and informal meetings – for every situation, such as the appropriately "cozy" library, the "shack" with vintage look for dynamic group work, the prestigious white boardroom for official meetings and the war room in anthracite. The new look supports both internal and external communication and strengthens identification with the rapidly growing company.

PROJECT FACTS **Location:** Schwedter Straße 263, 10119 Berlin, Germany. **Client:** Covus. **Completion:** 2012. **Gross floor area:** 1,200 m². **Type of business:** advertising agency.

MEETING PEOPLE — SBP – SEEL BOBSIN PARTNER

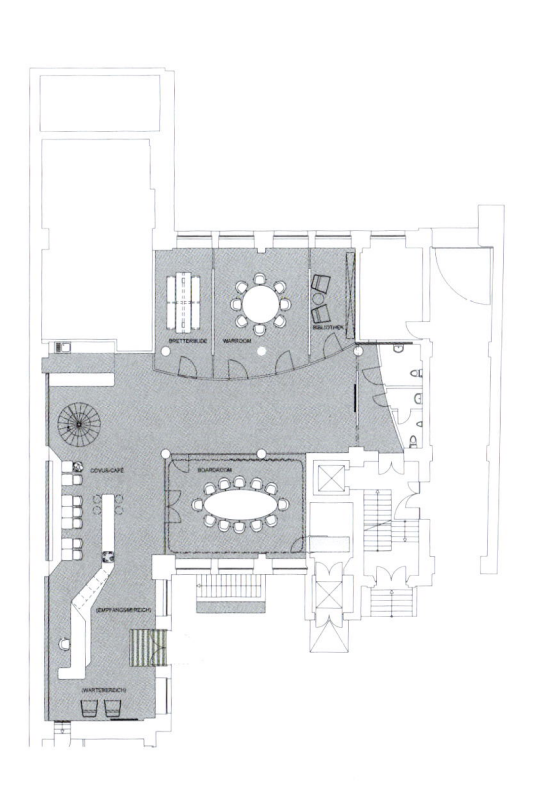

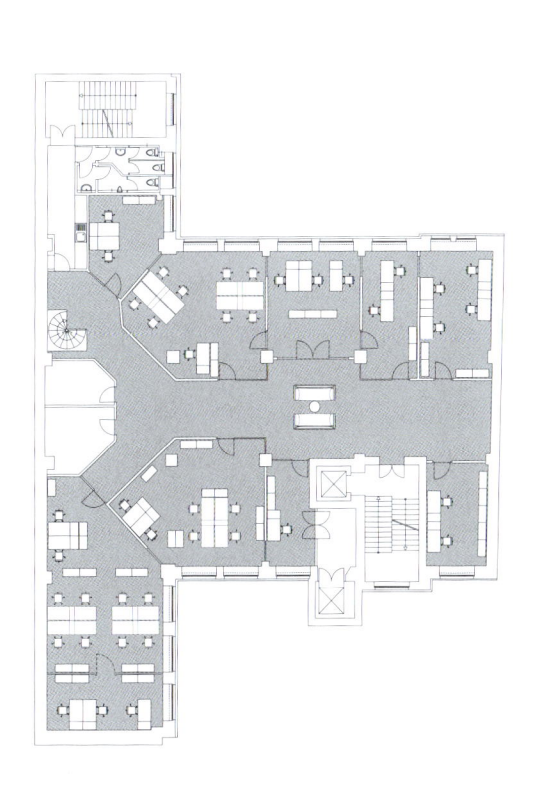

← ← | Covus bar
↖ | Meeting room
↑ | Corridor
↓ | Floor plans

MEETING PEOPLE | DH Liberty

↑ | **Interior view**, kitchen
→ | **Entrance hall**

Analog Folk

London

Converting a 930 square meters advertising agency called Analog Folk in Shoreditch was one of DH Liberty's first projects. Design Haus Liberty took on the task of infusing a traditional London building with sculptural modernism. The DH Liberty design opened up the building into a large, industrial loft-like working space. Adding a mezzanine and a new staircase enhanced the space in the building, and a glazed façade added character. Analog Folk's goal was to build an advertising agency that captures traditional methods people use to receive information, while tapping into new digital information technologies. Design Haus Liberty defined this goal architecturally by using reclaimed "found" objects and giving them a new life in the Analog Folk office.

PROJECT FACTS **Location:** Shoreditch, London, United Kingdom. **Design team:** Dara Huang, Lisa Hinderdael, Remo de Angelis, Ryan Day. **Contractor:** Mark Alexander. **Client:** Analog Folk. **Completion:** 2013. **Gross floor area:** 930 m². **Type of business:** advertising agency.

MEETING PEOPLE DH LIBERTY

↑ | **Conference room**
← | **Chandelier lamp,** with recycled bottles

ANALOG FOLK

↑ | Interior view
← | Floor plans

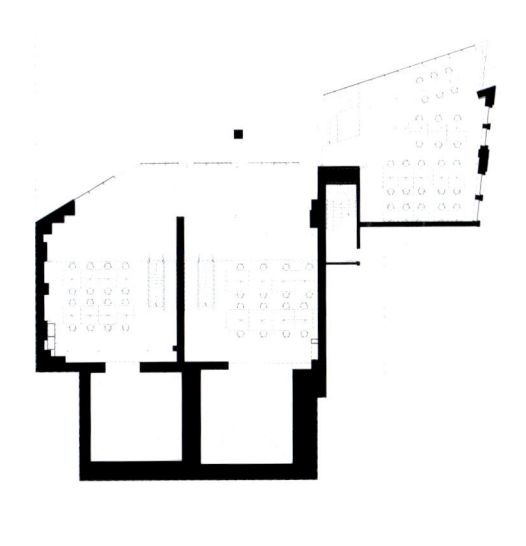

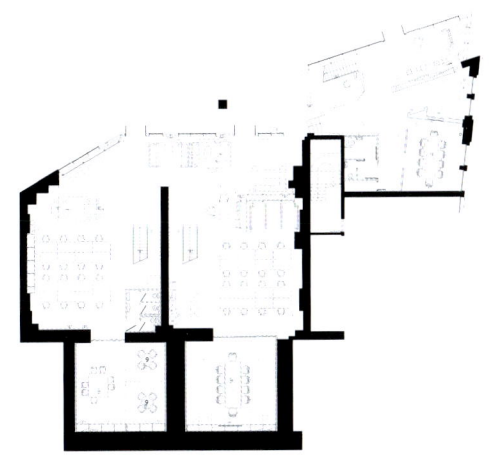

MEETING PEOPLE | Melbourne Design Studios

↑ | Trolleys at desks
↗ | Central island
→ | Double shopfront

Birkenstock Australia Headquarters

Melbourne

The result of cool contemporary design, with a warm feel and an holistic approach to sustainability is a series of spaces that are a joy to be and work in. The multi-award winning design succinctly translates the brand's core values into a spatial experience, intuitively illustrating Birkenstock's commitment to craftsmanship and quality, to health and sustainability. The run-down heritage building was restored to its former glory, extended and complemented by a contemporary fitout. The new headquarters consist of wholesale offices, workshop, courtyard, retail space, online store, and a warehouse with a newly inserted mezzanine as wholesale showroom.

PROJECT FACTS **Location:** 113-115 Queen's Parade, Clifton Hill, Melbourne, Australia. **Contractor:** emac constructions. **Completion:** 2013. **Gross floor area:** 500 m². **Type of business:** fashion.

MEETING PEOPLE MELBOURNE DESIGN STUDIOS

↑ | Plywood workshop
← | New workshop courtyard

BIRKENSTOCK AUSTRALIA HEADQUARTERS

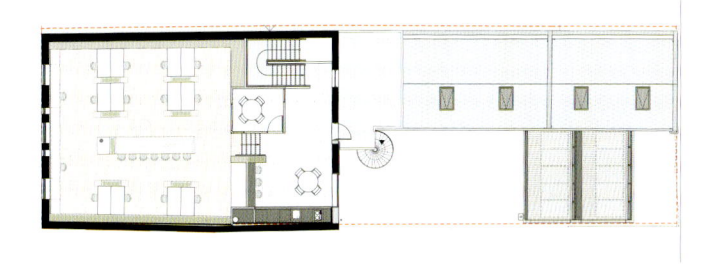

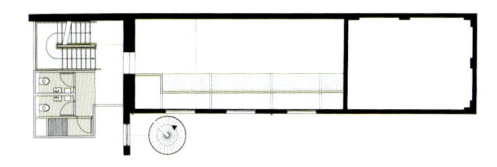

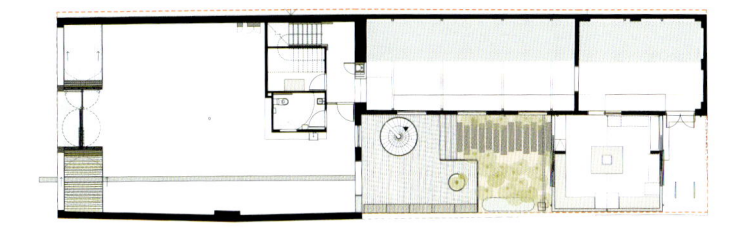

← | Mezzanine story
↑ | Floor plans
↓ | Warehouse

MEETING PEOPLE

estudio ji
(Jorge Frías + Irene Zurdo)

↑ | **Meeting room,** plug walls and shelves
→ | **Showroom,** interior view

Studio – Showroom & Gallery

Altea

The module "PLUG" is the result of an investigation of how to utilize space for activity which lasts for a short or long period of time. This activity, whether domestic or commercial, is always linked to a long list of functional Jond esthetic uses. It is perfect for habitat, commerce or retail. PLUG is a 190x90 centimeters mobile modular piece with several accessories designed and tailored to their anchoring system: "stick, table, chair, hang..." Inspired by traditional space partition screens, PLUG is a vertical series of lattices which, besides its obvious transparency, also serve as supports and anchorages for various accessories. The module works individually or in groups, adapting to any situation, shape or space.

PROJECT FACTS **Location:** Altea, Spain. **Architects and furniture designers:** Jorge Frías + Irene Zurdo. **Client:** private. **Completion:** 2013. **Gross floor area:** 48 m². **Type of business:** studio, showroom and gallery.

MEETING PEOPLE   ESTUDIO JI (JORGE FRÍAS + IRENE ZURDO)

↑ | **Showroom**, interior view
← | **Meeting room**, plug walls and shelves
↓ | **Section and floor plan**

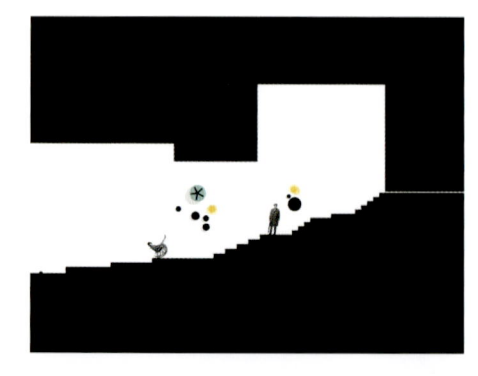

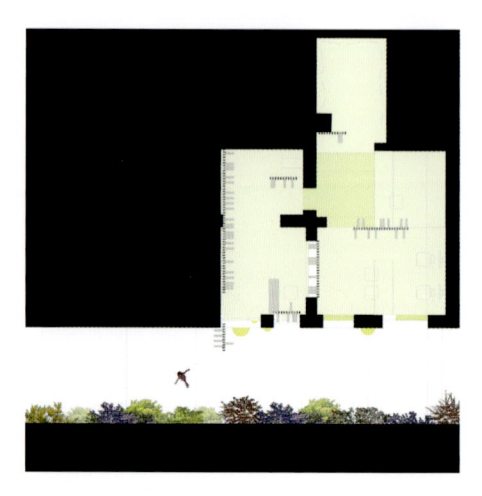

STUDIO – SHOWROOM & GALLERY

← | **Showroom**, interior view
↑ | **Axonometric view**
↙ | **Gallery view**
↓ | **Exterior view**

MEETING PEOPLE | +ADD

↑ | Space to create
↗ | Workstations
→ | Wooden platforms

FiftyThree

New York

FiftyThree is a space to create a combination between workspace, library, home and a forest. With that as a creed, a space was created that involved a very honest and open layout that promoted teamwork and collaboration. The selection of materials was walnut wood, blackened steel, glass, and concrete complemented by a couple of accents of marble. These became a palette to start drawing what became an office space that reflects the client's needs. A variation of spaces emerged that enhanced the everyday working experience, but also developed unknown or new ways of working. The result is a space that invites you to stay, share ideas and create the most amazing and well thought out products. Both the interior and exterior of the building, which is now one of the most important Internet hubs in the world, were designated New York City landmarks in 1991.

PROJECT FACTS **Location:** Tribeca, New York, USA. **Client:** FiftyThree, Inc. **Completion:** 2014. **Gross floor area:** 613 m². **Type of business:** hardware and software.

MEETING PEOPLE +ADD

↑ | Lounge area
← | Entry hall

FIFTYTHREE

↑ | Pantry
← | Floor plan
↓ | Section

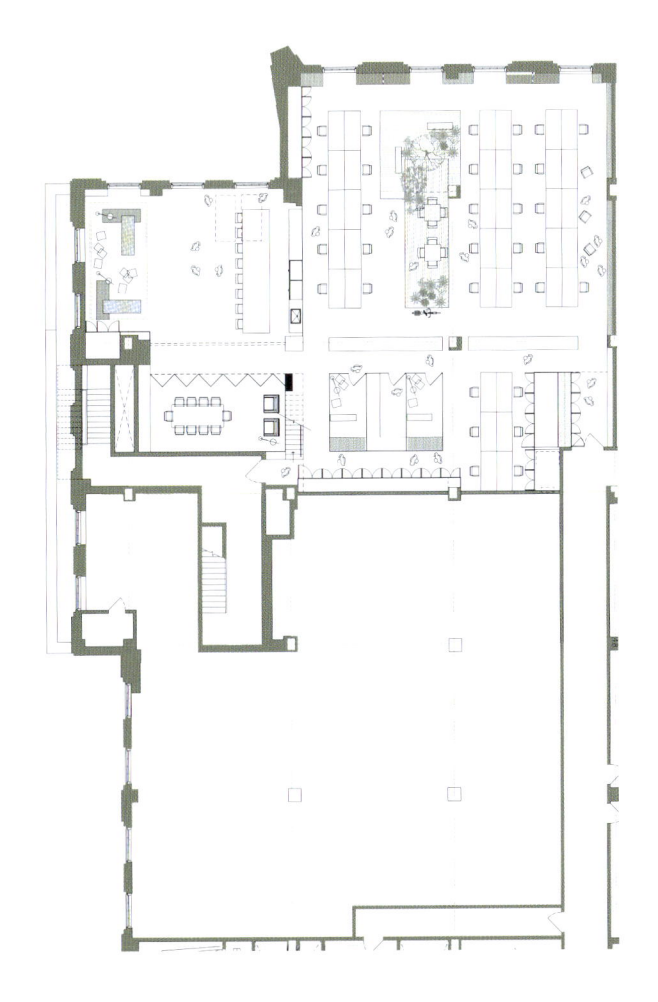

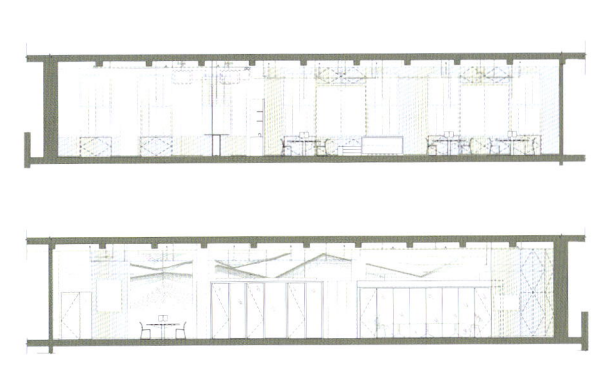

MEETING PEOPLE | GEREMIA DESIGN

↑ | Office view
↗ | Conference room
→ | Meeting space

Path Offices

San Francisco

The office is on the edge of downtown. For the path office, the office used a lot of the color red to match their brandingand also used a lot industrial materials. The inclusion of some quirky accessories inspired by the staff at Path. Many of the furniture pieces are custom, as well as the lighting. The layout of the space is very open plan. Geremia Design introduced tables instead of the typical cubical, in a pinwheel formation for individual privacy. Because of a long-term relationship with Path, the design of the office expands as the company expands. Germia Design established a relationship, so the office is trusted to take risks and experiment with materials. This has resulted in some incredible custom furniture and artwork.

PROJECT FACTS **Location:** San Francisco, CA, USA. **Client:** Path. **Completion:** 2012. **Gross floor area:** 930 m². **Type of business:** technology company.

MEETING PEOPLE   GEREMIA DESIGN

↑ | Conference room
← | Quirky accessories

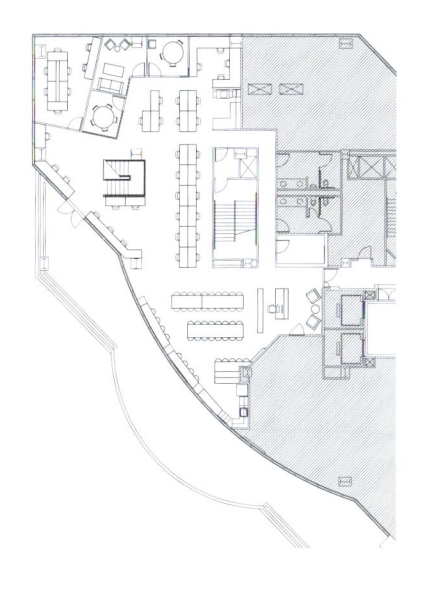

PATH OFFICES

← | Blackboard
↑ | Floor plan
↓ | Lounge area

MEETING PEOPLE | Baran Studio Architecture

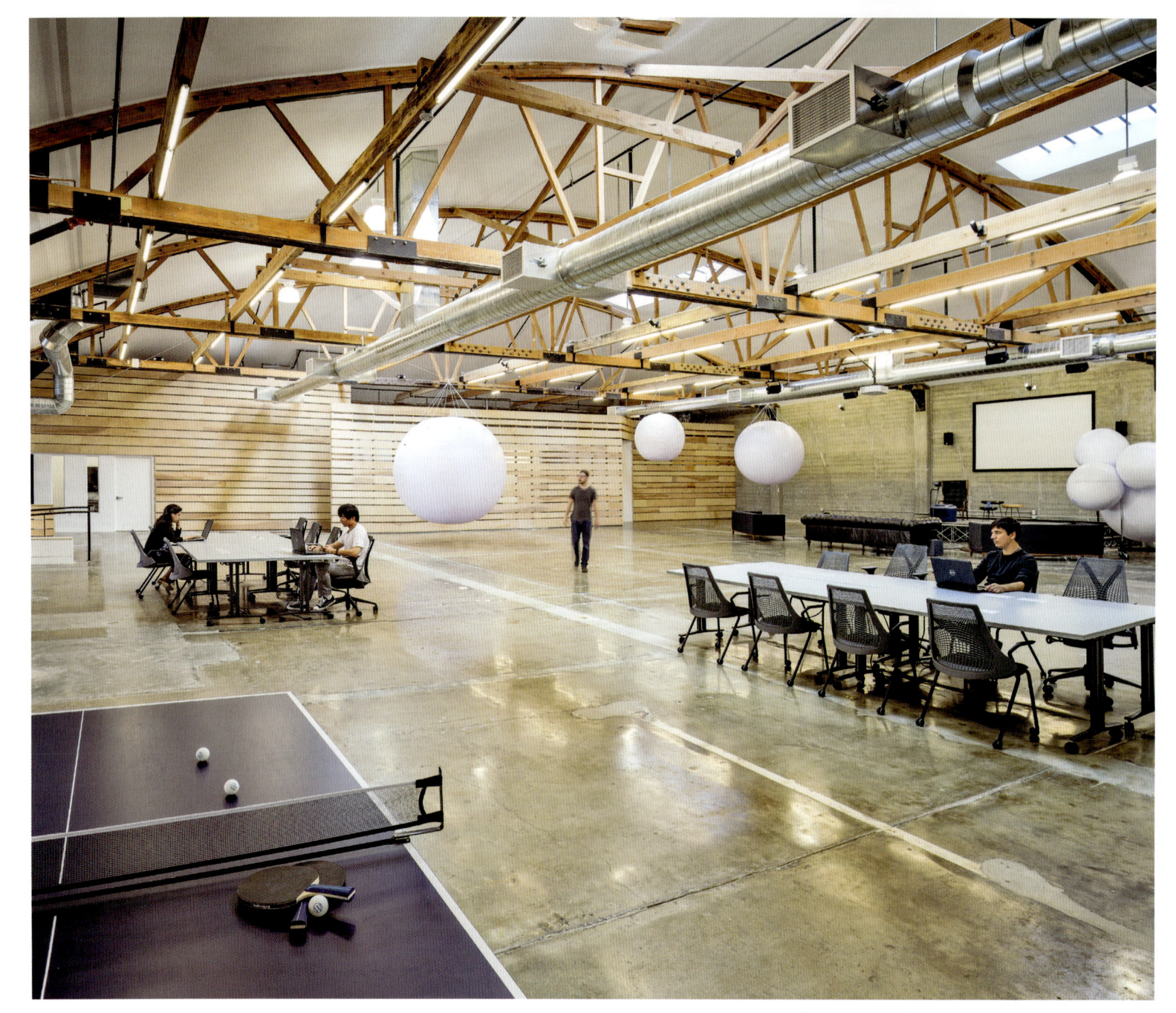

↑ | Open studio space
→ | Re-imagined warehouse

Wordpress Automattic Space

San Francisco

The Baran Studio task was to create a space that could accommodate the usual contingent of 15 to 20 people, but also accommodate a few hundred coders (who need to plug-in) for a special program or event. Wordpress's new Automattic Space is a re-imagined warehouse that was formerly a martial arts studio that had fallen into disrepair. The core concept for the transformation was to maintain the clarity and simplicity of the existing shell, and insert an adaptive new 'sleeve' or insert. The plywood wall winds throughout, guiding the visitor through the space. The wall serves several functional purposes along the way.

PROJECT FACTS

Location: Hawthorne Street, San Francisco, CA, USA. **Other creatives involved:** Darren McMurtrie. **Client:** Wordpress Automattic. **Completion:** 2013. **Gross floor area:** 1,324 m². **Type of business:** web development corporation.

MEETING PEOPLE

BARAN STUDIO ARCHITECTURE

↑ | Exhibition space
← | Staircase
↓ | Site plan

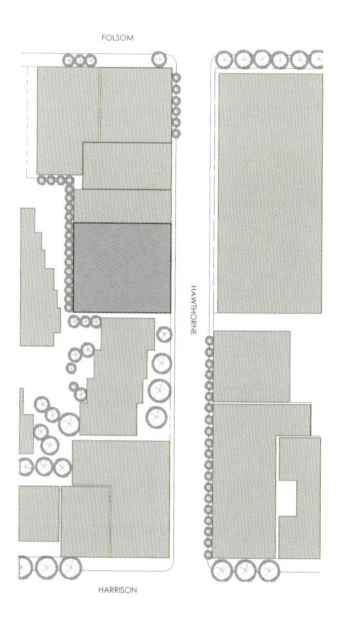

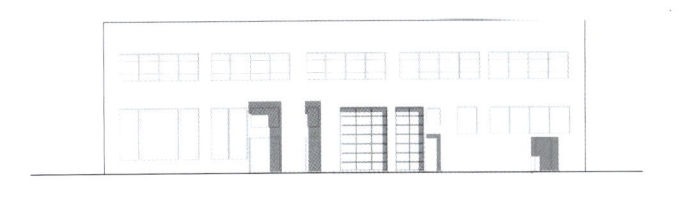

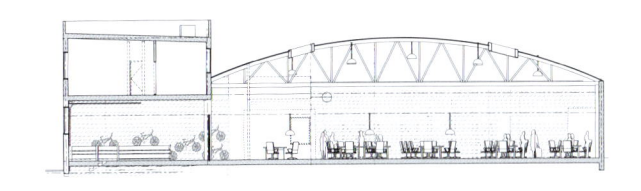

WORDPRESS AUTOMATTIC SPACE

← | Cafe
↑ | View and section
↓ | Lounge area

MEETING PEOPLE | Studio O+A

↑ | **First floor**, reception
→ | **Second floor**, lounge area with fireplace

Giant Pixel

San Francisco

Small space design, because of its inherent warmth and intimacy, sometimes offers opportunities not found in projects on a larger scale. O+A's design challenge at Giant Pixel was to fit a variety of distinct work areas into limited space – without sacrificing openness. The process began at the front door. Giant Pixel's reception area leads directly into work and meeting space, but is clearly defined by three unique features. First, a reception desk that looks more like a natural rock formation than a piece of furniture; next, a witty desk-lamp chandelier in contrast to, but oddly harmonious with the geological desk; and finally a blackened steel entrance canopy cut with a pattern of squares that conveys a readable message to programmers schooled in the code.

PROJECT FACTS **Location:** 431 Jessie Street, San Francisco, CA 94103, USA. **Client:** Giant Pixel. **Completion:** 2013. **Gross floor area:** 390 m². **Type of business:** technology company.

MEETING PEOPLE   STUDIO O+A

↑ | **Conference room and break area**
← | **Basement,** conference room

GIANT PIXEL

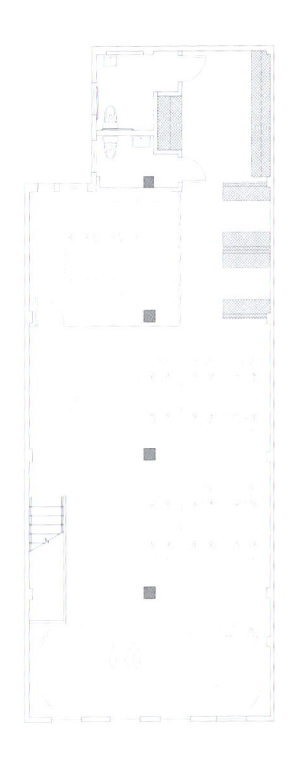

← | **Basement**, lounge banquette seating
↑ | **Floor plans**
↓ | **Second floor**, lounge

MEETING PEOPLE | HDG Architecture

↑ | Office space
↗ | Lounge area
→ | Conference room

HDG Architecture's Office

Spokane

The project involved the interior and exterior renovation of a 1930s building in a downtown revitalization zone in Spokane, Washington. HDG Architecture is a multifaceted architecture and design studio with experience in commercial, residential, hospitality and restaurant design. Architecture, interior design, branding and graphic design are all in house assets affording HDG Architecture the level of control required for their pursuit of an integrated, cohesive and appealing design solution.

PROJECT FACTS **Location:** Spokane, Washington, USA. **Client:** HDG Architecture. **Completion:** 2013. **Gross floor area:** 102 m². **Type of business:** commercial and residential architecture, interior design, marketing and branding.

MEETING PEOPLE   HDG ARCHITECTURE

HDG ARCHITECTURE'S OFFICE

←← | Interior view
↑ | Open office
← | Floor plan

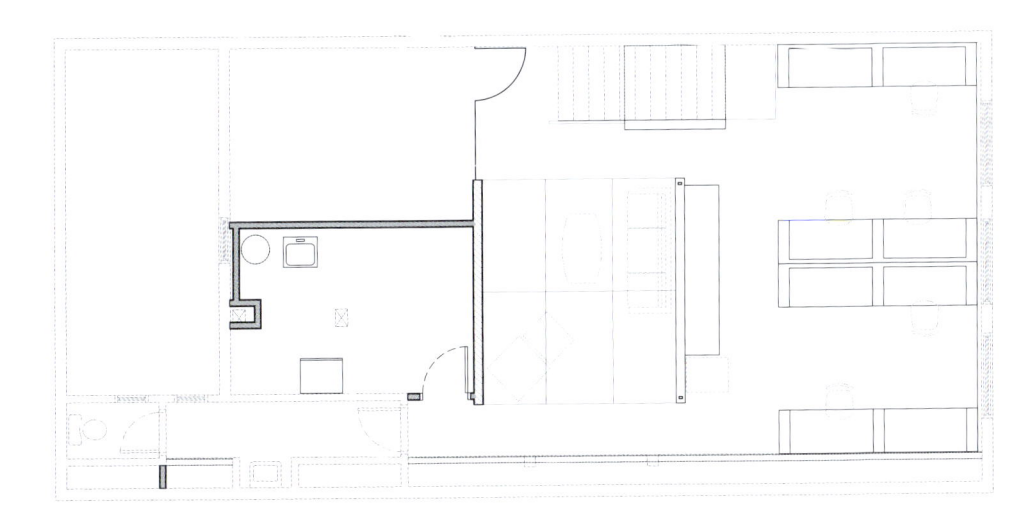

MEETING PEOPLE | nuvolaB architetti associati

↑ | **Mezzanine workspace**
↓ | **Workspace**, three options

↗ | **Meeting room**
→ | **Front view**, wooden cabinet

3Logic MK Corporate HQ

Pisa

The computer company 3Logic MK reorganized its headquarters in the heart of the historic center of Pisa, reusing the space of the old rectory in the church of San Frediano. The place encompasses a linear succession of four spaces: a hall, a large room, a small room and some storage spaces characterized by high ceilings. The natural light comes from the large windows in the upper part of the south wall, facing the cloister. However these conditions and the historical ambiance didn't permit a rational management and distribution of the functions, according to the needs of the client. Thus the new office is entirely designed around a large furniture unit housing the required functions: an archive, a small lab, and walls with office equipment and shelves.

PROJECT FACTS **Location:** Via San Frediano 5, 56126 Pisa, Italy. **Project leader:** Nicola Lariccia. **Client:** 3Logic MK. **Completion:** 2012. **Gross floor area:** 135 m². **Type of business:** digital manufacturing.

MEETING PEOPLE   NUVOLAB ARCHITETTI ASSOCIATI

↑ | Reception
← | Section and floor plan

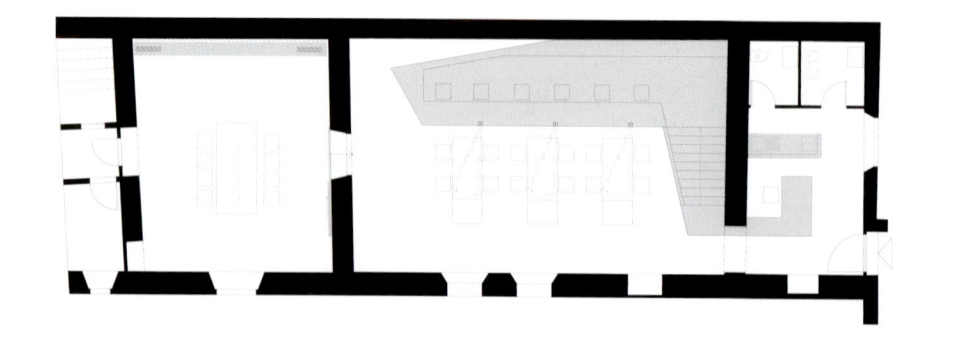

3LOGIC MK CORPORATE HQ

↑ | **General view**, workspace
← | **Entrance**
↓ | **Isometry**

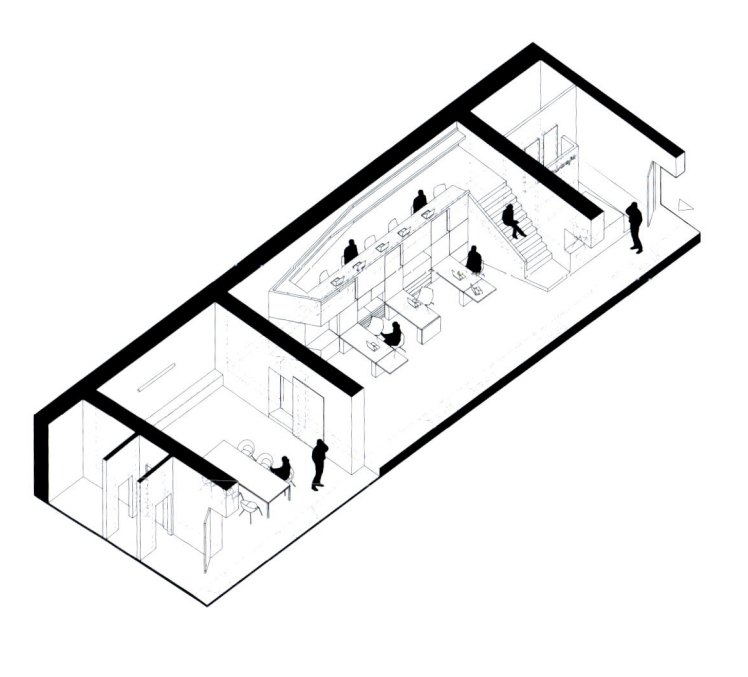

MEETING PEOPLE | SCOPE
office for architecture

↑ | **Façade view**
↗ | **Cafeteria area**
→ | **Break room,** to hang out

Innovation Center

Potsdam

The building located on Jungfernsee lake provides a creative workspace for 100 employees and 200 students, supporting innovative and efficient mix between customers, researchers and students. Using an open floor plan, 30 employees per zone are provided all the functions needed for daily work. In order to quickly and simply modify team collaboration a system with track mounted whiteboards was introduced. The latest insights in innovation management were incorporated in the conception and design of the building. In particular concepts from Silicon Valley and the School of Design Thinking in Stanford were adopted. The selection of unfinished materials like polished screed floors, exposed concrete, untreated wood and exposed installations transmits deliberately the character of a workshop, recalling the origins of software development in start-ups.

PROJECT FACTS **Location:** Konrad-Zuse-Ring 10, 14469 Potsdam, Germany. **Architect and contractor:** SCOPE office for architecture. **Completion:** 2013. **Gross floor area:** 4,500 m². **Type of business:** software development.

MEETING PEOPLE SCOPE OFFICE FOR ARCHITECTURE

↑ | **Variable teamspace**
← | "Living Room"

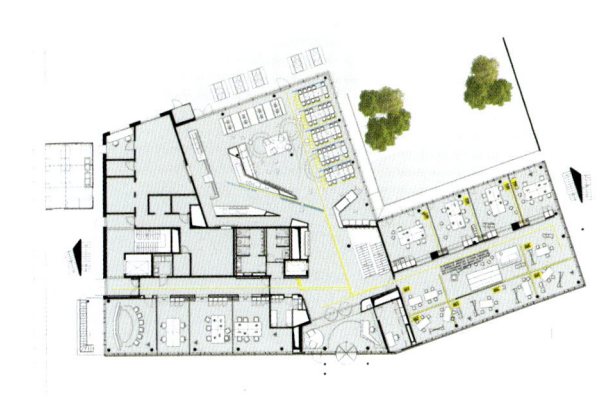

INNOVATION CENTER

← | **Collaboration room**, for short meetings
↑ | **Plan**
↓ | **Design lab**, with whiteboards

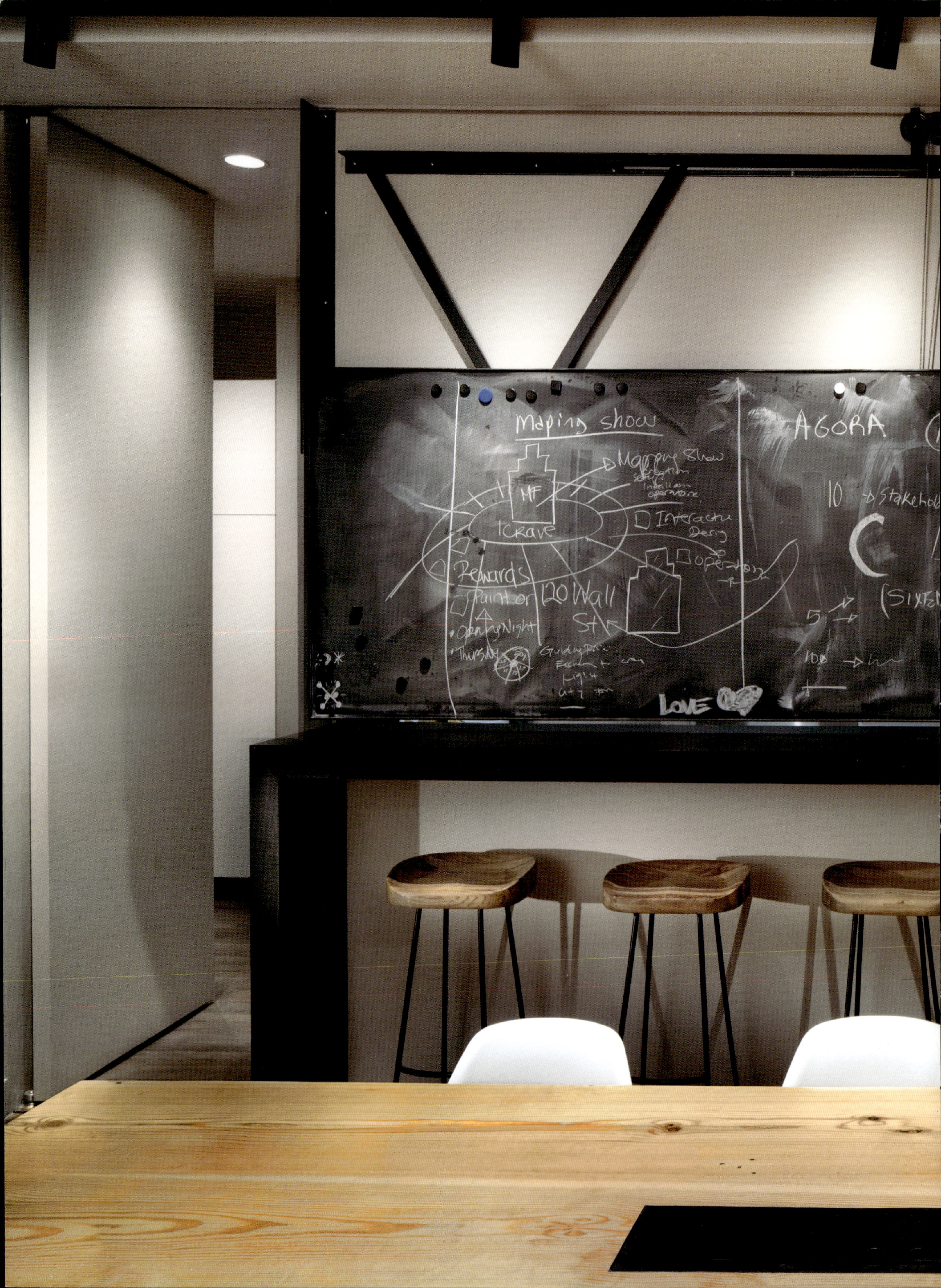
Maping show
AGORA
MF
iCrave
Rewards
120 Wall St
LOVE

BUILDING CONCEPTS

BUILDING CONCEPTS | pS Arkitektur

↑ | **Work area**, bookshelf
→ | **Lounge**

Dynabyte

Stockholm

pS Arkitektur has created a fun and playful new interior for Dynabyte located in central Stockholm, Sweden. The design scheme was evolved around the theme of the early stages of the Internet. The walls are decorated with custom-made Ascii-art, which is art composed of programming text. Abstracted out of this color scheme, a meta-realistic design theme is applied on photo realistic wallpapers. The rooms are designed with themes like sea, forest and city. A kind of meta concept where nothing is what it seems to be, quite like the digital world itself where nothing is 'for real' but exists because it depicts the real world. Kitchen tiles, doors and even objects are all part of the masquerade that plays a part in this new and spirited concept.

PROJECT FACTS **Location:** Kammakargatan, Stockholm, Sweden. **Client:** Dynabyte. **Completion:** 2010. **Gross floor area:** 1,400 m². **Type of business:** information technology.

BUILDING CONCEPTS   PS ARKITEKTUR

↑ | **Office**
← | **Workspace**

← | Meeting area
↓ | Meeting rooms

BUILDING CONCEPTS | ICRAVE

↑ | **Conference room,** with sliding doors
↗ | **Reception desk,** doubles as DJ booth
→ | **Doors,** convert to private conference room

ICRAVE Office

New York

After rapid growth, ICRAVE, a New York-based experiential branding and design firm, made the move to an 8,000-square-foot studio with the intention of really making it their own. The space, designed by the team itself, goes beyond the notion of an open plan office – it is designed specifically to foster ICRAVE's immersive, collaborative culture. The design process was a collective effort of the entire studio. Dream sessions were held to harvest ideas, where team members examined different areas, giving everyone a chance to bring their ideas to the table. Among the options, ICRAVE then crowd-sourced the best solution for each micro-environment, and created a one-of-a-kind office. The result is a truly collaborative office space that fosters employees' creativity and interaction.

PROJECT FACTS **Location:** 1140 Broadway 1st Floor, New York, USA. **Client:** ICRAVE. **Completion:** 2012. **Gross floor area:** 740 m². **Type of business:** design firm.

BUILDING CONCEPTS　　　ICRAVE

↑ | **Open studio**
← | **Entrance,** with custom mural and archery target

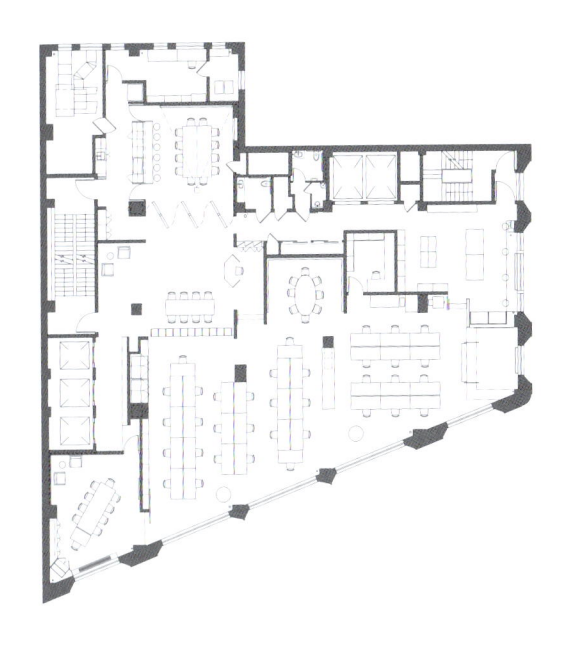

ICRAVE OFFICE

← | Additional work surfaces
↑ | Floor plans
↓ | Raised chalkboard, creates kitchen bar

BUILDING CONCEPTS | GIRALDI ASSOCIATES ARCHITECTS

↑ | Project room
→ | Reception

Giraldi Associates Architects Headquarters

Florence

Giraldi Associates Architects have relocated their headquarters in Florence inside the palazzo Antinori-Aldobrandini in a space of about 600 square meters. Plaster and frescoes combine perfectly with the fresh and modern design, creating a truly unique workplace. The atmosphere is new, exciting, young and dynamic, thanks to the spaces that define a strong communication and design identity. The structure is divided into eleven areas, including rooms dedicated to design, materials testing and meeting rooms. There is also a kitchen that gives colleagues the opportunity to interact during breaks and a relaxation area with a green carpet that recalls the color of grass.

PROJECT FACTS **Location:** Via dei Serragli 9, Florence, Italy. **Client:** GIRALDI ASSOCIATES ARCHITECTS. **Completion:** 2013. **Gross floor area:** 600 m². **Type of business:** architecture studio.

BUILDING CONCEPTS   GIRALDI ASSOCIATES ARCHITECTS

↑ | Reception
← | Project room

GIRALDI ASSOCIATES ARCHITECTS HEADQUARTERS

↑ | Project room
← | Meeting room
↓ | Floor plan

BUILDING CONCEPTS | de Winder Architects

↑ | **Interior view,** through the editorial space
→ | **Reception counter,** with wooden plank back wall

Zeit Online Editorial

Berlin

An open space with communication enhancing sightlines was designed for the online edition of "Zeit" in a sprawling row of shops in Berlin-Kreuzberg. The four editorial management offices are housed as a free-standing glass box within the space. The completely glass enclosed single office in the front offers an unencumbered view of the central news desk and the departments. The line lights emphasize the length of the hallways. A reception area with striking counter, a break and lounge space with kitchenette, guest offices, conference rooms, as well as four cubicles as retreats for individual work fill out the editorial space.

PROJECT FACTS

Location: Askanischer Platz 1, 10963 Berlin, Germany. **Wall painting color in the event area "Farbvorfall":** Peter Möller. **Client:** Zeit Online. **Completion:** 2012. **Gross floor area:** 1,300 m². **Type of business:** editorial.

BUILDING CONCEPTS DE WINDER ARCHITECTS

↑ | Entrance area
← | Break room with kitchenette
↗ | Event room
→ | Editor-in-chief's office
→→ | Floor plan

ZEIT ONLINE EDITORIAL

217

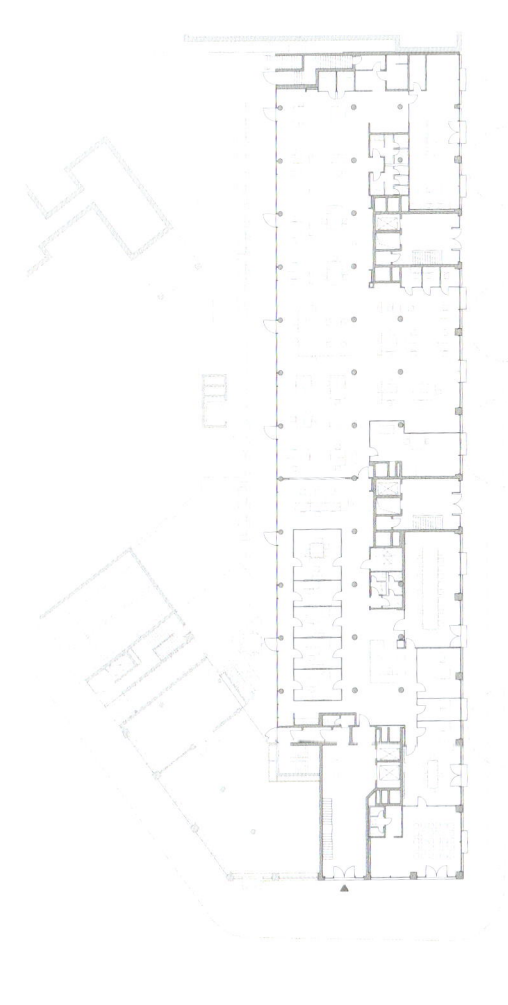

BUILDING CONCEPTS | Snook Architects

↑ | **Entrance hall,** with feature wall
↓ | **Studio view**

↙ | **Kitchen**
↓ | **Interior view**
↗ | **Lounge area**
→ | **Entry hall**

Uniform

Liverpool

Uniform's work is eclectic in approach responding to individual clients requirements in a surprising and often unexpected way. Their new office is a physical realization of this working method characterized by the ever changing media wall that acts as both a seperation from the reception area to the studio space beyond. Rather than a complete physical barrier the wall offers tantalizing views to the work being done beyond and acts as a platform to present work to potential clients. The overall palette of materials used in the project continues the inventive philosophy utilizing everyday utilitarian fabrics in unexpected situations.

PROJECT FACTS **Location:** Bold Street, Liverpool, United Kingdom. **Client:** Uniform. **Completion:** 2013. **Gross floor area:** 650 m². **Type of business:** new media.

BUILDING CONCEPTS	SNOOK ARCHITECTS

↑ | **Conference room**
← | **Plywood**

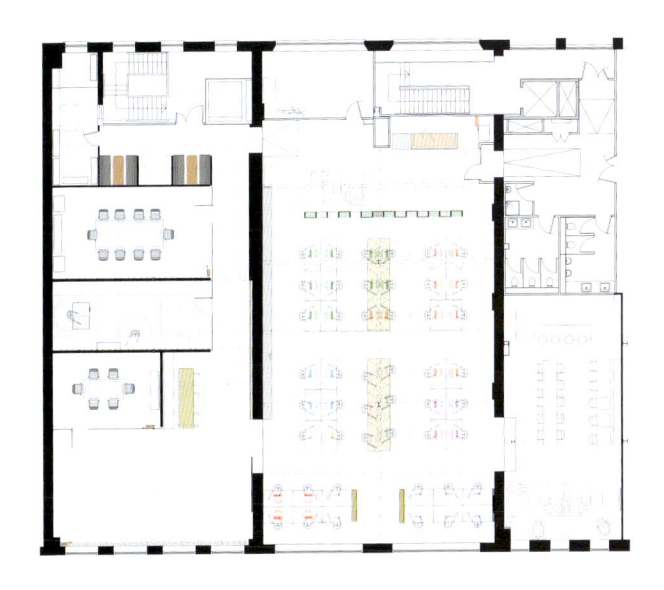

UNIFORM

↑ | Kitchen
← | Studio
↓ | Floor plan

BUILDING CONCEPTS | Okidoki arkitekter AB

↑ | **Interior view,** workspace
↗ | **Office space,** with people working

Nudie Jeans Headquarters

Gothenburg

Nudie Jeans headquarters is located in Antikhallarna in Gothenburg, a house built in 1885 for on behalf of Skandinaviska Banken. The old historic premises in Neo-Renaissance style was renovated and rebuilt in 2011. Okidoki had 1,500 square meters, spread over the top two floors of the house, to make into the Nudie Jeans new home. Nudie moved there in February 2012. Okidoki wanted to highlight both the uniqueness of the Nudie brand and the historical building, and let the old premises interact with the core of what Nudie Jeans stands for and represents. The basic idea was, in full accordance with Nudie philosophy, to "keep what was worn and fix what was broken." As the Nudie Jeans office, it had to reflect that philosophy both internally and externally.

PROJECT FACTS
Location: Gothenburg, Sweden. **Client:** Nudie Jeans company AB. **Completion:** 2012. **Total area:** 1,500 m².
Type of business: clothing brand.

BUILDING CONCEPTS   OKIDOKI ARKITEKTER AB

NUDIE JEANS HEADQUARTERS

←← | Waiting area
↑ | Main space
← | Reception area
↓ | Floor plan

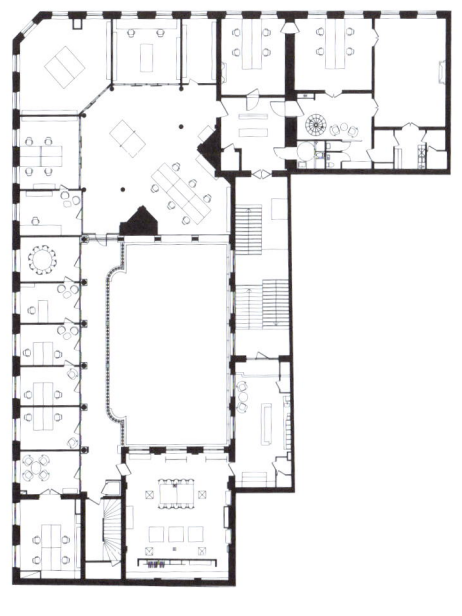

BUILDING CONCEPTS | Reaktioneins Guido Meier
Ralf Bender Design

↑ | **Conference room,** view from outside
↗ | **Entrance area**
→ | **Conference room,** with curtains

Komdat

Munich

Office-Traffic: Reflecting materials from the traffic on the street crop up in the form of ornaments on the surfaces of walls, the floor and furnishings, ordering in an unconscious way the various office sectors. For instance, "please come in", "here is the wardrobe" "please wait here", and so on. Work areas for management, division leaders, customer service and the reception are clearly demarcated by wood surfaces. The spatially opened server area provides an opportunity to interrupt the 2-dimensional guide system in order to create a piece of useful, 3-dimensional furniture in the form of a work surface.

PROJECT FACTS **Location:** Munich, Germany. **Completion:** 2005. **Gross floor area:** 1,200 m². **Type of business:** online marketing.

BUILDING CONCEPTS REAKTIONEINS GUIDO MEIER / RALF BENDER DESIGN

↑ | Entrance
← | Office

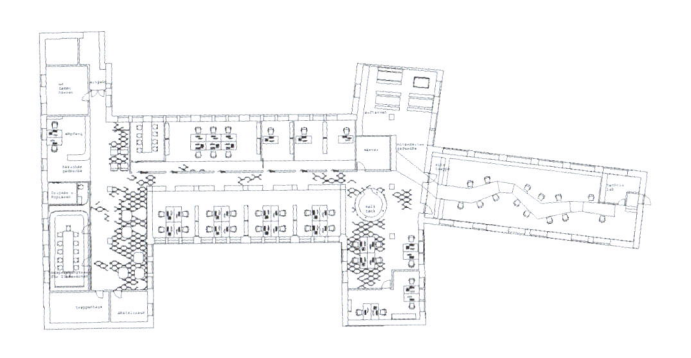

KOMDAT

← | Wardrobe
↑ | Floor plan
↓ | Desk

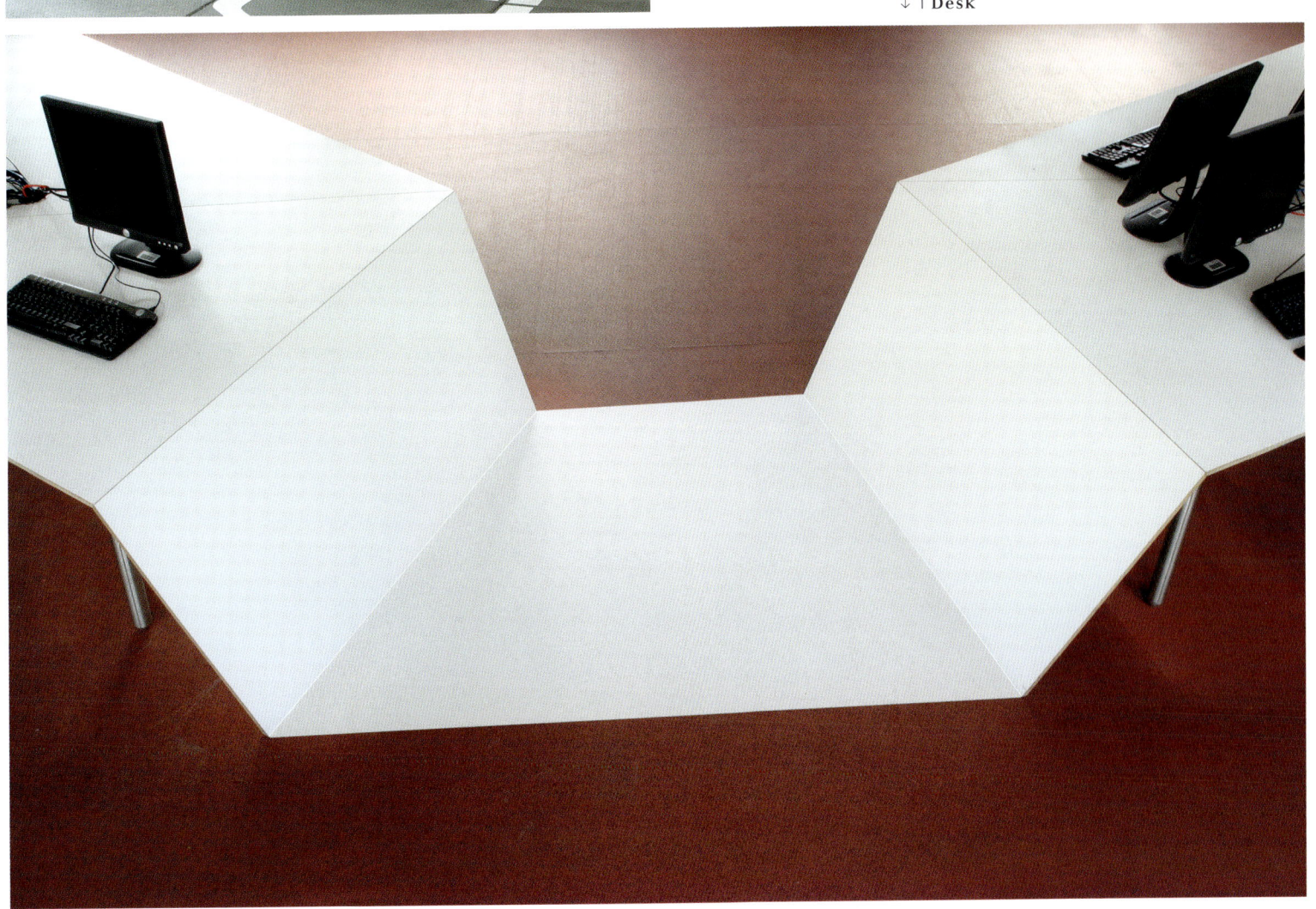

BUILDING CONCEPTS | Boris Voskoboinikov

↑ | Cafeteria
→ | Interior view

BBDO Group

Moscow

The main challenge that faced Nefaresearch's architects was to reconstruct a four-story 19th century factory building for the office of an advertising agency. The style of the office had to resemble an art centre, rather than a traditional office. The aim was to create a rich dynamic and contemporary image in the BBDO's (network of advertising agencies) branded palette (red, white, grey and black), covering and unifying all office spaces while dividing them into functional zones. The image also aims to provoke creative and unconventional. Chief Architect and founder of the studio – Boris Voskoboinikov – suggested defining the ground floor as a showcase, displaying the company image from the street and making the front group a powerful style-forming center. His concept perfectly reflected the nature of the BBDO Group.

PROJECT FACTS   **Location:** Moscow, Russia. **Client:** BBDO GROUP, Moscow. **Completion:** 2013. **Gross project area:** 3,400 m². **Type of business:** advertising agency.

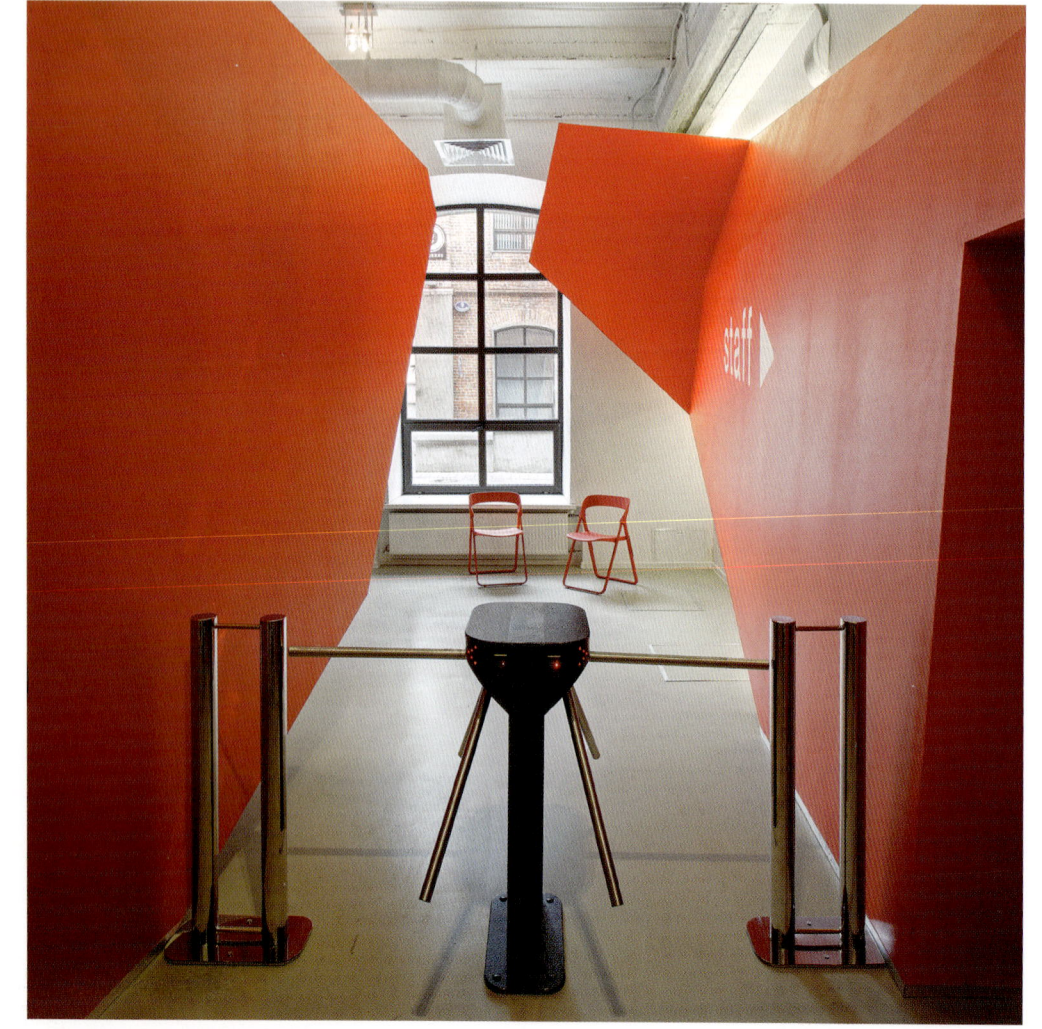

BUILDING CONCEPTS BORIS VOSKOBOINIKOV

↑ | Hall
← | Entrance

BBDO GROUP

↑ | Cafeteria
← | Room sculpture
↓ | Floor plan

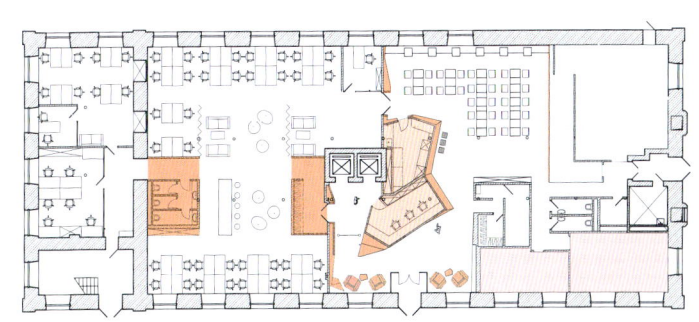

BUILDING CONCEPTS | Bestor Architecture

↑ | **Central work zone,** balance of vintage and modern furniture
↗ | **Conference room**
→ | **Photo studio**

Nasty Gal Headquarters

Los Angeles

Nasty Gal is a global online destination for fashion-forward, free-thinking girls. In 2006, founder Sophia Amoruso started an eBay store selling a highly curated selection of vintage pieces. In just five short years, the shop has grown to become an international style source offering both new and vintage clothing, shoes, and accessories. The name was inspired by the song and album "Nasty Gal". Bestor Architecture's challenge was to create one, cohesive creative office spanning three stitched together historic buildings in the heart of downtown Los Angeles. The design included preserving historic architectural elements such as cast concrete-clad trusses, brick, steel windows, concrete columns, marble flooring while stripping the existing cellular, subdivided space to open up and accommodate an egalitarian/democratic workspace and floor plan.

PROJECT FACTS   **Location:** Los Angeles, CA, USA. **Workplace and technical consultant:** Loescher + Meachem Architects. **Client:** Nasty Gal. **Completion:** 2014. **Gross floor area:** 3,901 m². **Type of business:** fashion.

BUILDING CONCEPTS   BESTOR ARCHITECTURE

NASTY GAL HEADQUARTERS

←← | The hub
↑ | Graphics and design area
← | Quiet work area

BUILDING CONCEPTS | Undercurrent Architects

↑ | **Exterior view**
→ | **Staircase,** with skylight

Archway Studios

London

Archway Studios is a live-workspace built in and around a 19th century rail viaduct. The project works with the constraints of an inner-city, industrial site next to a train line, and the challenges of a design that engages its surroundings. The building subverts tight site conditions, transforming a narrow plot with limited access to light, aspect and views, into an uplifting space that offers respite in spite extreme constraints. The building's unique design and appearance helps it to stand out even when dwarfed by inner-city neighbors. As one of 10,000 arches that dissect neighborhoods across London, it is a model that can be adapted to the benefit and benefit regeneration of the community.

PROJECT FACTS **Location:** Elephant and Castle, Southwark, London, United Kingdom. **Client:** private. **Completion:** 2012. **Gross floor area:** 160 m². **Type of business:** photographer studio.

BUILDING CONCEPTS UNDERCURRENT ARCHITECTS

← | Skylight detail
↓ | Exterior view

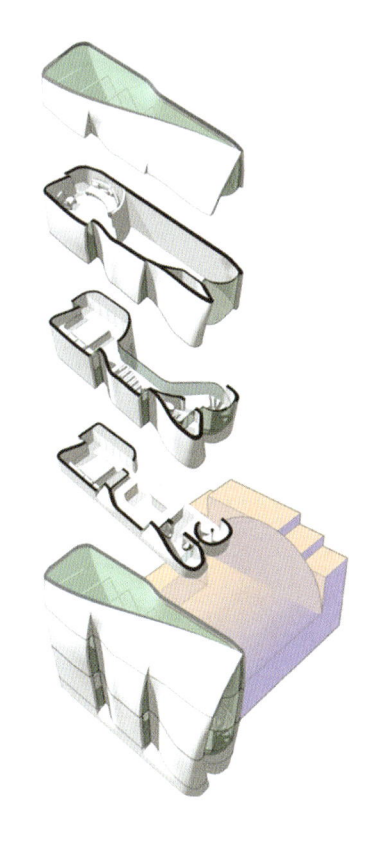

ARCHWAY STUDIOS

← | **Interior view**, office space
↑ | **Building scheme**
↓ | **Aerial view**, staircase

BUILDING CONCEPTS | TeamLab Architect

↑ | **Corridor**
↗ | **Interior view,** main desk
→ | **Bird's-eye view**

Pixiv Office

Tokyo

The idea behind Pixiv is to build a platform for everyone who enjoys illustration and to support work in Pixiv by bringing people together. Work can happen anywhere in the office. The production process occurs during discussions while showing a mock-up and moving hands. This process is important, therefore, space is provided for casual communication, an office environment where work can happen in the middle of a conversation. The 250-meters-work desk is not partitioned, with no clear definition of personal space. The employees will build the somewhat ambiguous space by themselves.

PROJECT FACTS **Location:** Tokyo, Japan. **Client:** Pixiv Inc. **Completion:** 2013. **Gross floor area:** 818 m². **Type of business:** online community for artists.

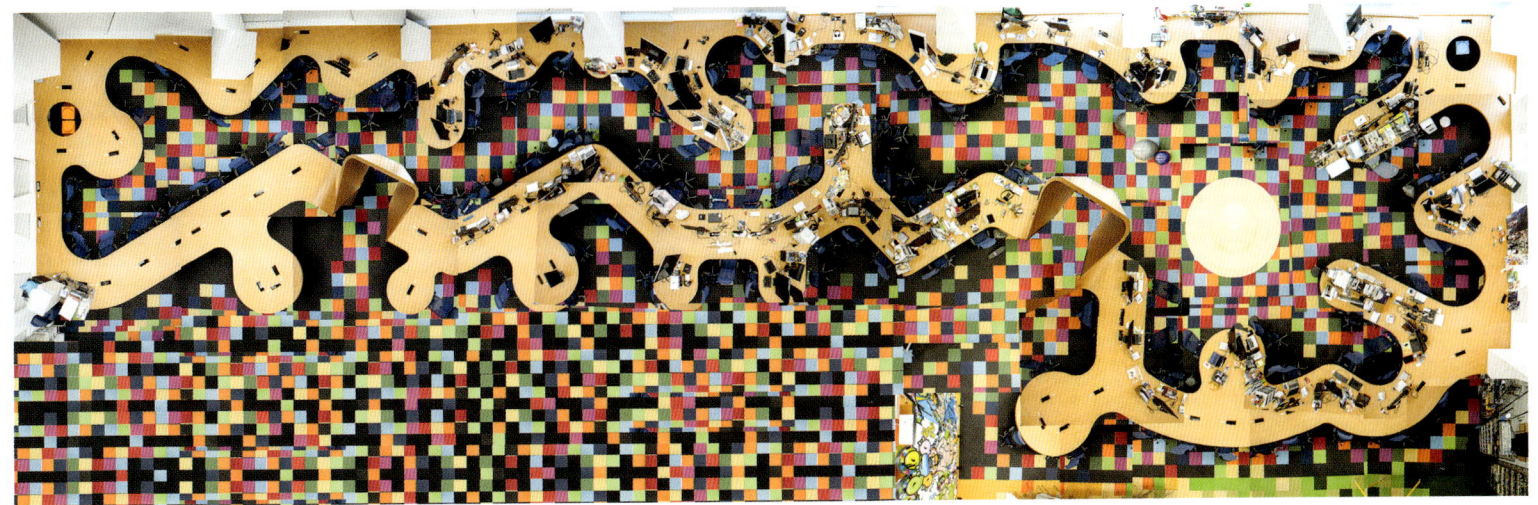

BUILDING CONCEPTS TEAMLAB ARCHITECT

↑ | General view
← | Detail of the table

PIXIV OFFICE

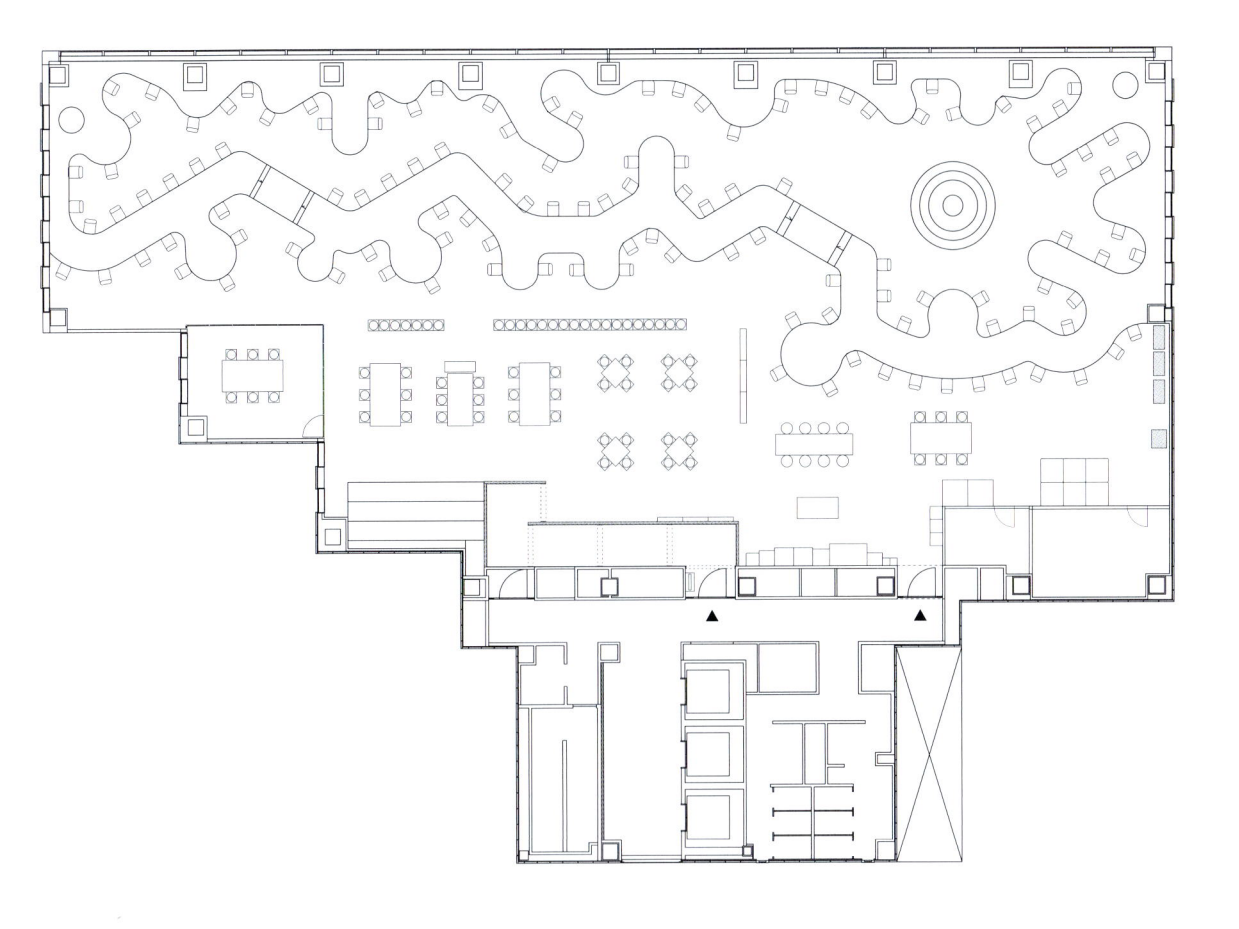

↑ | Floor plan
↓ | Passage under the worktable

BUILDING CONCEPTS | Hadi Teherani AG
Hadi Teherani Interior GmbH

↑ | **Meeting space,** the focus of concentration in discussions and brainstorming
→ | **Long view,** over the entire roof surface to the Elbe

Hadi Teherani Headquarters

Hamburg

The headquarters of the Hadi Teherani Group is the Lofthaus am Elbberg in Hamburg designed in 1994 – in the immediate vicinity of the awards winning buildings Dockland and Elbberg Campus. The interior shown here is from a renovation done in 2011. Architecture, interior design, product design and consulting for all communication and organizational functions are in one perfectly meshed building which is still individually responsive on different levels. Both upper floors in the glass roof, with a view of the Elbe and the harbor provide a direct reference for the interior design competence in an inspiring spatial continuum. This is where Hadi Teherani creates comprehensive and complex designs, from those with an innovative urban approach, to emotional architecture, to interiors defined down to the level of atmospheric detail.

PROJECT FACTS **Location:** Elbberg 1, 22767 Hamburg, Germany. **Interior design:** Hadi Teherani. **Completion:** 2011. **Gross floor area:** 400 m². **Type of business:** design & interior design.

BUILDING CONCEPTS   HADI TEHERANI AG / HADI TEHERANI INTERIOR GMBH

HADI TEHERANI HEADQUARTERS

←← | **Light and perspective,** at Elbberg
↑ | **Front desk**
← | **Library**
↓ | **Floor plans**

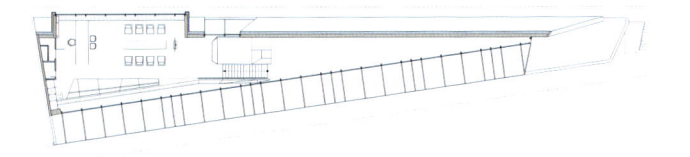

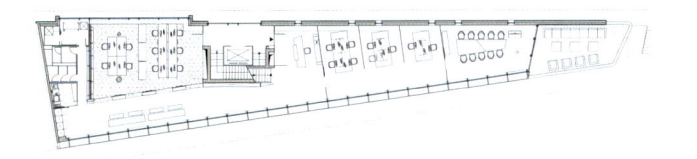

BUILDING CONCEPTS | Morpho Studio

↑ | Entrance hall
→ | Conference room

Pride and Glory Interactive Head Office

Cracow

The industrial character of the Zabłocie district where many factories and industrial plants were situated goes much further back than the mid-19th century. In this setting, in a building of a former cable factory, the head office of the Pride and Glory Interactive agency is located. The interior has been fitted with elements such as award display shelves made of ladders, woodwork inspired by details found in barns, shelves, the reception desk and some of the tables made of lumber from the demolition of a 100-year-old house. The post-industrial space turned out to be the perfect background for original furniture and accessories softening the austerity of the building and enhancing the qualities of the interior.

PROJECT FACTS **Location:** Cracow, Poland. **Client:** Pride and Glory Interactive. **Completion:** 2012. **Gross floor area:** 810 m². **Type of business:** advertising agency.

BUILDING CONCEPTS · MORPHO STUDIO

→ | Lounge area
← | Lamp

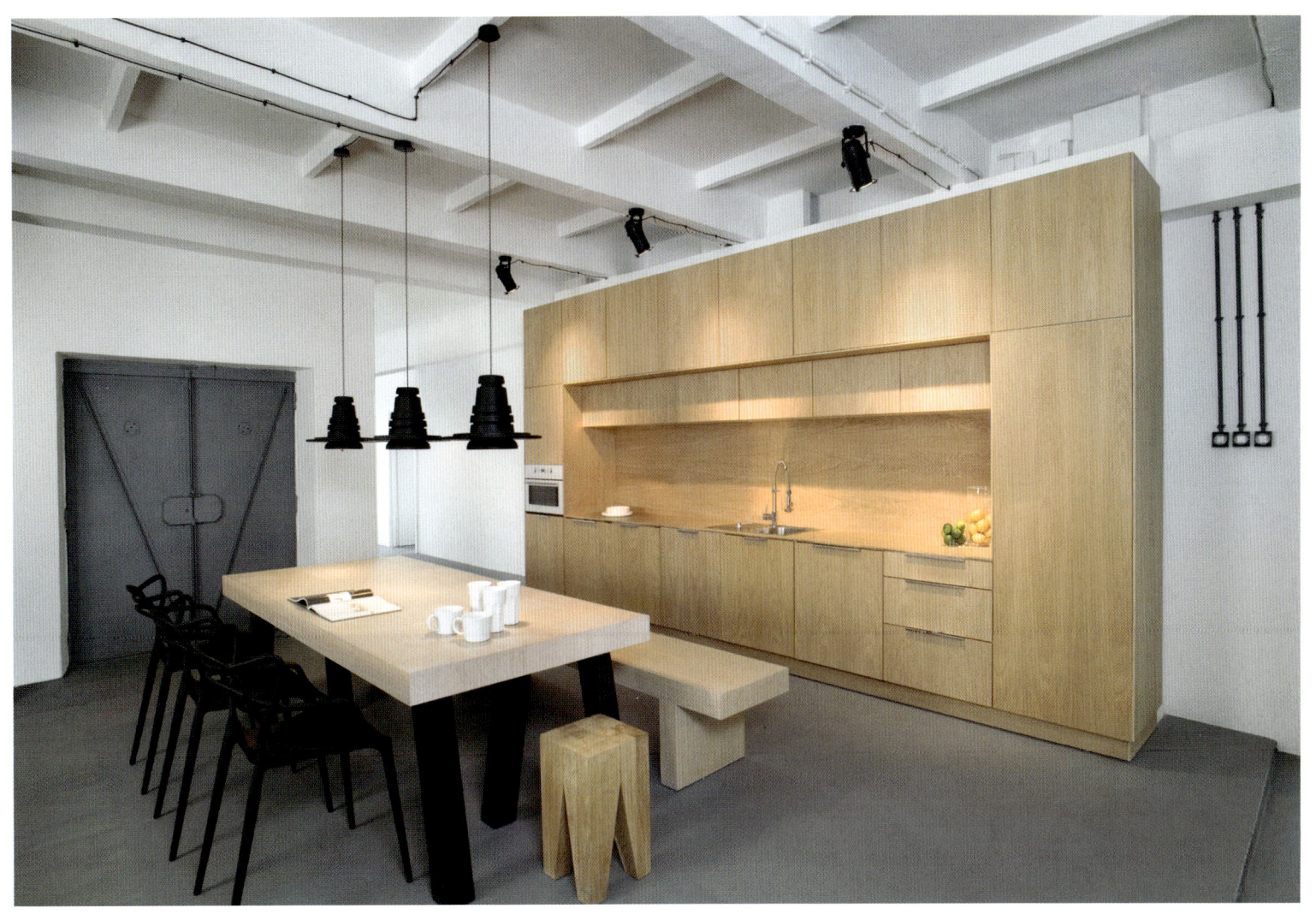

PRIDE AND GLORY INTERACTIVE HEAD OFFICE

↑ | Conference room
← | Chandelier lamp
↓ | Floor plans

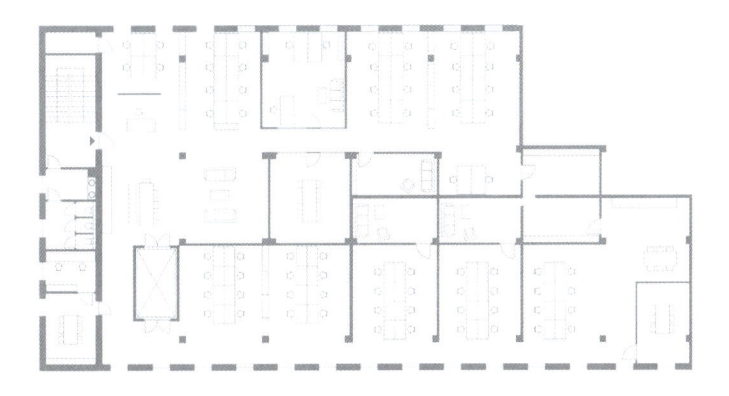

BUILDING CONCEPTS | Architectural studio M17

↑ | Office room
↗ | Workspace
→ | Coffee-point

V-Confession Agency Office

Moscow

The V-Confession Office is located in the historical part of Moscow close to Ostozhenka Street. It occupies the fourth floor of the old mansion. At that time it was decorated with cheap traditional office solutions such as suspended ceilings and painted wallpaper. In the process of clearing the space a number of different materials turned up – brick, concrete blocks and wooden rib walls. Concerning the historical value of this building, some construction elements were exposed and the original decorative elements such as parquet, plaster moldings were saved. The stylistic preference for office space is minimalism. The architectural method of perimeter white background is widely used for exhibition spaces. The diagonal volume shifting is inspired by V-Confession corporative style graphics which also provides the basis for the office geometry, including furniture such as metal tables and bookshelves.

PROJECT FACTS **Location:** 2y Obydenskiy Pereulok, Moscow, Russia. **Client:** V-Confession Agency. **Completion:** 2013. **Gross floor area:** 156 m². **Type of business:** creative agency.

BUILDING CONCEPTS   ARCHITECTURAL STUDIO M17

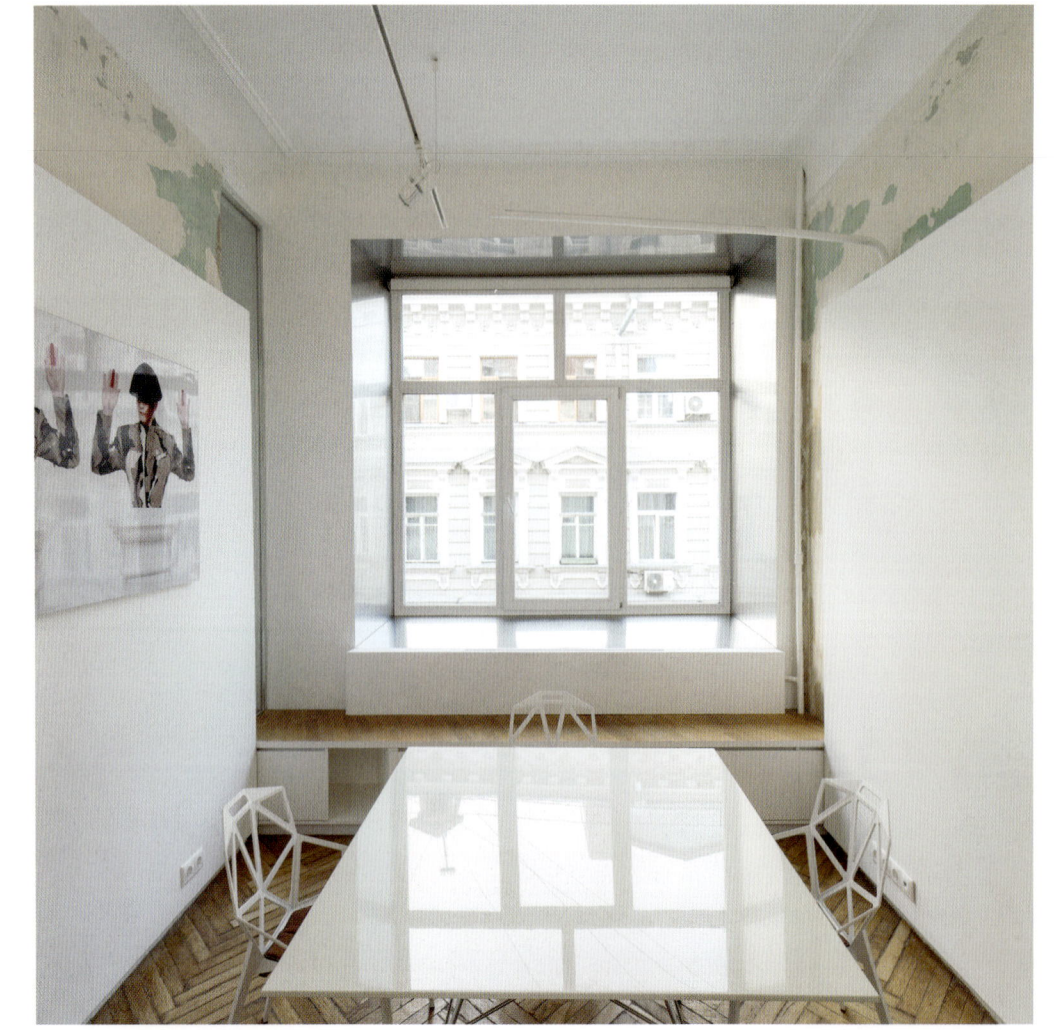

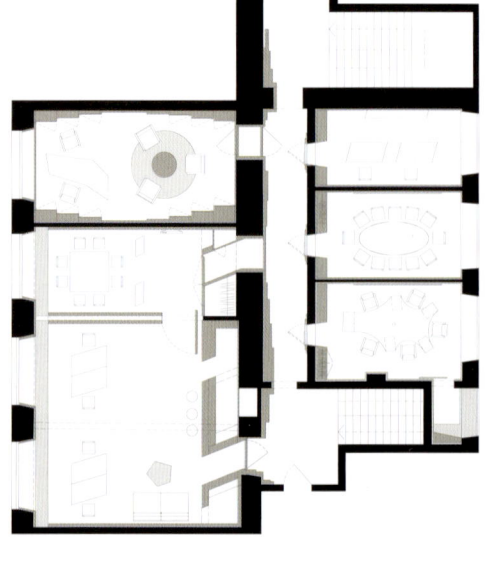

↑ | Executive office
← | Meeting room
↓ | Floor plan

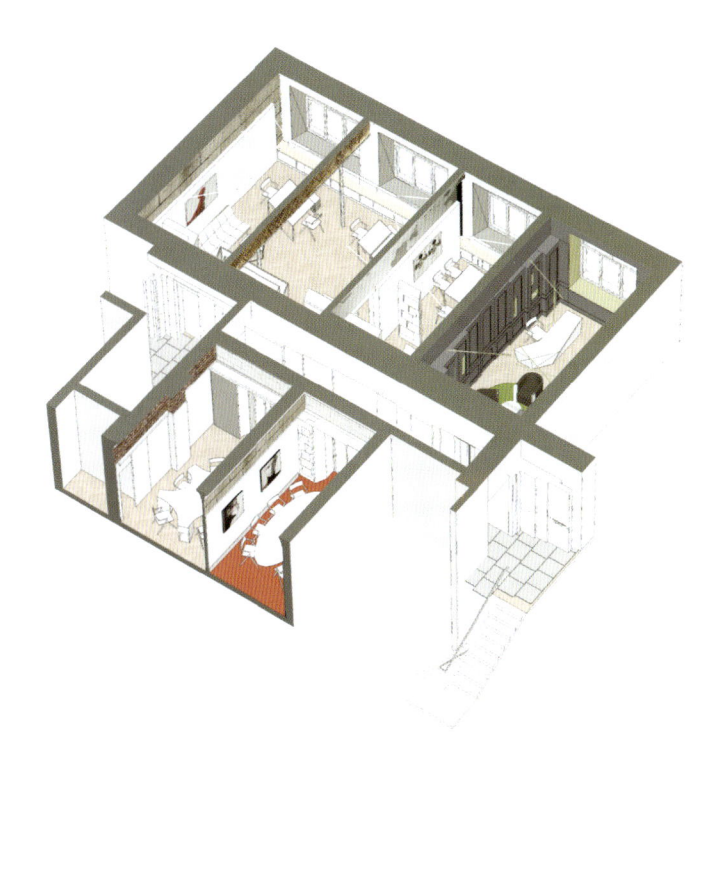

V-CONFESSION AGENCY OFFICE

← | Meeting room
↑ | Section scheme
↓ | Executive office, detail

BUILDING CONCEPTS | MAKE Creative

↑ | Open office space
↗ | Conferece room
→ | Kitchen, breakout

Unit B4 Office

Sydney

The property group, Goodman, engaged MAKE to develop a concept for the adaptive re-use of an existing warehouse in Alexandria. The space was to house Goodman's South Sydney team; functioning at the same time as a marketing showcase for Goodman clients. The brief was to create a contemporary office space within an industrial shell, working with the raw and unfinished qualities of the space, as well as addressing scale and proportion. MAKE responded to the large volume of the space in a sculptural way, developing a series of large simple plywood boxes to house the meeting rooms, amenities, and form the entry to the space. The bathrooms were designed as a contrast to the workspace; dark and graphic, reusing 44 gallon drums to create sinks and bins. Custom wallpaper panels layer industrial photography with colored graphics.

PROJECT FACTS **Location:** Alexandria, Sydney, Australia. **Builders:** Intermain. **Designers:** MAKE Creative. **Completion:** 2012. **Gross floor area:** 375 m². **Type of business:** property development.

BUILDING CONCEPTS   MAKE CREATIVE

UNIT B4 OFFICE

←← | Entry hall
↑ | Meeting
← | Studio
↓ | Floor plan

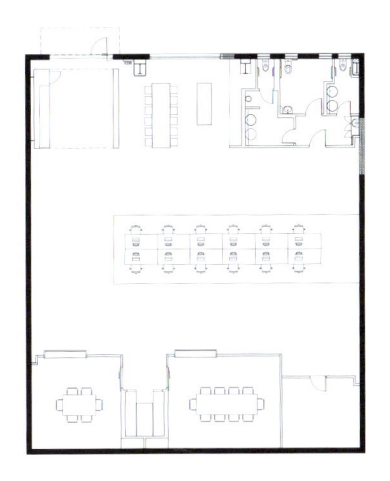

Index Archi

tects' Index

ARCHITECTS' INDEX

+ADD

155 Water Street, Suite 613
New York, 11201 (USA)
T +1.1.212.777.1874
info@plusadd.org
www.plusadd.org

→ 172

Architectural studio M17

Chistoprudniy Bulvar 23 c2
Moscow (Russia)
T +7.926.531.17.76
17masterskaya@gmail.com
www.m17architects.com

→ 254

Assemble Studio

20 High Street
Northcote VIC 3070 (Australia)
T +61.3.9939.6789
hello@assembleprojects.com.au
www.assembleprojects.com.au/

→ 32

Baran Studio Architecture

5621 Lowell Street
Oakland, 94608 (USA)
T +1.510.415.710.0486
mbaran@mbarchitect.net
www.baranstudio.com/

→ 180

Bestor Architecture

3920 Fountain Avenue
Los Angeles, 90029 (USA)
T +1.323.666.9399
hey@bestorarchitecture.com
www.bestorarchitecture.com

→ 50, 234

Boora Architects

720 SW Washington, Suite 800
Portland, OR 97205 (USA)
T +1.503.226.1575
info@boora.com
www.boora.com

→ 144

Boris Voskoboinikov

127015, B.Novodmitrovskaya st. 36, bld 12
Moscow (Russia)
T +7.499.504.42.46
pr@nefaresearch.ru
www.nefaresearch.ru

→ 230

Corvin Cristian

3, pictor Stahi Street
Bucharest (Romania)
T +40.213.141.458
corvin@corvincristian.com
www.corvincristian.com

→ 90

Design Blitz

435 Jackson Street
San Francisco, 94111 (USA)
T +1.415.525.9179
info@designblitzsf.com
www.designblitzsf.com

→ 122

Designliga

Hans-Preißinger-Straße 8 / Halle A
81379 Munich (Germany)
T +49.89.624.219.40
hello@designliga.com
www.designliga.com

→ 60

de Winder Architects

Schlesische Straße 26
10997 Berlin (Germany)
T +49.30.61.77.69.80
info@dewinder.de
www.dewinder.de

→ 214

DH Liberty

125A Westbourne Grove
W24UP London (United Kingdom)
T +44.020.7998.8274
info@dhliberty.com
www.dhliberty.com

→ 160

DOS Architects

17-19 Lever Street
EC1 V3QU London (United Kingdom)
T +44.207.253.8222
dos@dosarchitects.com
www.dosarchitects.com

→ 148

Ector Hoogstad Architecten

Laanslootseweg 1
3028 Rotterdam (The Netherlands)
T +31.10.440.21.21
info@ectorhoogstad.com
www.ectorhoogstad.com

→ 130

Eriksen Skajaa Architects

St. Halvards Plass 1
0192 Oslo (Norway)
T +47.936.942.11
post@eriksenskajaa.no
www.eriksenskajaa.no

→ 72

esludio ji

Travesía de San Miguel, 1
Altea, Alicante (Spain)
T +34.676.973.501
info@estudioji.com
www.estudioji.com

→ 168

Fraher Architects Ltd.

London SE231DT
London (United Kingdom)
T +44.20.829.169.47
mail@fra-her.com
www.fra-her.com

→ 64

GEREMIA DESIGN

6480 Vallejo Street
Emeryville, 94608 (USA)
T +1.510.92.28.904
info@geremiadesign.com
www.geremiadesign.com

→ 176

GIRALDI ASSOCIATES ARCHITECTS

Via dei Serragli 9
50124 Florence (Italy)
T +39.055.219.132
studio@giraldiassociati.it
www.giraldiassociati.it

→ 210

Hadi Teherani AG & Hadi Teherani Interior GmbH

Elbberg 1
22767 Hamburg (Germany)
T +49.40.444.054.3
design@haditeherani.com
www.haditeherani.com

→ 134, 246

HDG Architecture

522 W 1st Avenue
Spokane, 99201 (USA)
T +1.509.321.5064
Josh@studiohdg.com
www.studiohdg.com

→ 188

ARCHITECTS' INDEX

Holst Architecture

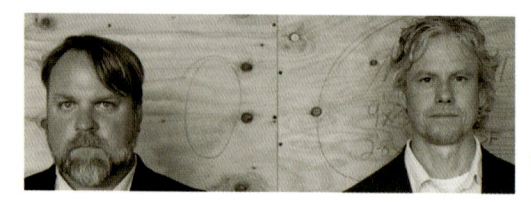

110 SE 8th
Portland, 97214 (USA)
T +1.503.233.9856
mail@holstarc.com
www.holstarc.com

→ 102

ICRAVE

1140 Broadway 1st Floor
New York, 10001 (USA)
T +1.212.929.5657
info@icrave.com
www.icrave.com

→ 206

Jean de Lessard, creative designers

7091, 8e avenue Montréal
H2A 3C5 Québec (Canada)
T +1.514.729.2732
info@delessard.com
www.delessard.com

→ 56

KINZO Berlin

Leipziger Straße 61
10117 Berlin (Germany)
T +49.30.814.522.520
info@kinzo-berlin.de
www.kinzo-berlin.de

→ 78

KNOL

Linnaeusparkweg 160
1098 EN Amsterdam (The Netherlands)
T +31.634.148.155
info@storiesbyknol.com
www.storiesbyknol.com

→ 12

MAKE Creative

583 Elizabeth Street
Sydney (Australia)
antonia@make.net.au
www.make.net.au

→ 258

Melbourne Design Studios

33 Montgomery Street
3081 Heidelberg Heights (Australia)
T +61.3.9077.2240
Welcome@MelbourneDesignStudios.com.au
www.MelbourneDesignStudios.com.au

→ 164

Morpho Studio

ul. Przemysłowa 12
30701 Krakow (Poland)
T +48.506.148.268
justyna@morphostudio.pl
www.morphostudio.pl

→ 250

MOST Architecture

Westzeedijk 399
3024 EK Rotterdam (The Netherlands)
T +31.6.4515.2688
info@mostarchitecture.com
www.mostarchitecture.com

→ 42

Neri&Hu Design and Research Office

88 Yuqing Road
200030 Shanghai (China)
T +86.21.6082.3777
info@neriandhu.com
www.neriandhu.com

→ 82

nuvolaB architetti associati

Viale E.De Amicis 99/a
50137 Florence (Italy)
T +39.055.933.45.15
mail@nuvolab.it
www.nuvolab.it

→ 192

Okidoki arkitekter AB

Kastellgatan 1
S41307 Gothenburg (Sweden)
T +46.31.352.46.60
info@okidokiarkitekter.se
www.okidokiarkitekter.se

→ 222

Oppenheim Architecture+Design Europe and Huesler Architekten

Kirchplatz 18
4132 Muttenz (Switzerland)
T +41.61.378.93.03
beat@oppenoffice, huesler@hueslerarchitekten.ch
www.oppenoffice.com, www.hueslerarchitekten.ch

→ 46

Origins Architecture

Schieweg 210
2636 KA Schipluiden (The Netherlands)
T +31.10.477.81.31
info@origins-architecten.nl
www.origins-architecten.nl

→ 24

Particular

912/365 Little Collins Street
3000 Melbourne (Australia)
T +61.3.9942.3082
admin@particular.ch
www.particular.ch

→ 118

People's Architecture Office

Qihelou South Alley, Yard No. 8
100006 Beijing (China)
T +86.114.246.10
office@peoples-architecture.com
www.peoples-architecture.com

→ 28

Peter Sampson Architecture Studio

707 Sara Avenue
Winnipeg, R3G0Y8 (USA)
T +1.204.475.9323
studio@psastudio.ca
www.psastudio.ca

→ 94

Peter Stasek Architects–Corporate Architecture

Werderstraße 40
68165 Mannheim (Germany)
T +49.151 50.400.900
info@stasek.de
www.stasek.de

→ 98

Petokraka

Kralja Milutina 30
Belgrade (Serbia)
T +38.111.414.816.0
milica@petokraka.com, aleksa@petokraka.com
www.petokraka.com

→ 126

PL.ARCHITEKCI

Ul. Dlugosza 13/12
Poznan (Poland)
T +48.61.223.71.39
biuro@plarchitekci.pl
www.plarchitekci.pl

→ 152

pS Arkitektur

Kvarngatan 14
118 47 Stockholm (Sweden)
T +46.8.702.06.30
info@psarkitektur.se
www.psarkitektur.com

→ 202

ARCHITECTS' INDEX

Reaktioneins / Ralf Bender Design

Elsässer Straße 24
81667 Munich (Germany)
T +49 89 954 834 95
guido@reaktioneins.com
www.reaktioneins.com

→ 226

sbp - Seel Bobsin Partner

Rostocker Straße 16
20099 Hamburg (Germany)
T +49.40.25.49.45.54
info@sbpdesign.de
www.sbpdesign.de

→ 156

SCOPE office for architecture

Römerstraße 32
70180 Stuttgart (Germany)
T +49.711.215.7384.0
info@scopeoffice.de
www.scopeoffice.de

→ 196

selgascano

C/ Guecho 27. sc
28023 Madrid (Spain)
T +34.913.076.481
selgascano1@gmail.com
www. selgascano.net

→ 20

Simon Bush-King Architecture & Urbanism

Ruysdaelkade 91
1072 Amsterdam (The Netherlands)
T +31.06.816.085.36
info@simonbushking.com
ww.simonbushking.com

→ 114

SKA Sibylle Kramer Architekten

Fettstraße 7a
20357 Hamburg (Germany)
T +49.40.432.789.6
mail@kramer-architekten.de
www.kramer-architekten.de

→ 86

Snook Architects

Unit 256, 5-9 Slater street
L1 4BW Liverpool (United Kingdom)
T +151.707.0100
neil@snookarchitects.com
www.snookarchitects.com

→ 218

Stephen Williams Associates

Admiralitätsstraße 71
20459 Hamburg (Germany)
T +49.40.879.334.00
mail@stephenwilliams.com
www.stephenwilliams.com

→ 68

studio mk27 – Marcio Kogan + Gabriel Kogan

Alameda Tiete 505
01417-020 São Paulo (Brazil)
T +55.11.3081.3522
info@studiomk27.com.br
www.studiomk27.com.br

→ 36

Studioninedots

Krelis Louwenstraat 1, b28
1055 ka Amsterdam (The Netherlands)
T +31.204.889.269
info@studioninedots.nl
www.studioninedots.nl

→ 110

Studio O+A

452 Tehama Street
San Francisco, 9410 (USA)
al@o-plus-a.com
www.o-plus-a.com

→ 106, 184

TeamLab Architect

Tosetsu Hongo Bldg. 5F, 1-11-6
113-0033 Tokyo (Japan)
T +81.3.5804.2356
www.team-lab.net

→ **242**

Those Architects

9/17 Thurlow Street
2016 Redfern (Australia)
T +61.414.494.837
gday@thosearchitects.com.au
www.thosearchitects.com.au

→ **140**

Tsutsumi & Associates Nie Yong

Room 1005, Tower14, Jianwai SOHO, No 39, the East
Beijing (China)
T +86.135.5273.2435
tsutsumi@tsuaa.com
www.tsuaa.com

→ **16**

Undercurrent Architects

Southwark
London (United Kingdom)
T +44.786.644.00.66
info@undercurrent-architects.com
www.undercurrent-architects.com

→ **238**

PICTURE CREDITS

Anichini, Francesca	210-213	Hobhouse, Jack	64-67	PAO, Beijing	28-31
Appelhof, Petra	130-133	Holst Architecture	102-105	PARTICULARCH PTY LTD, Melbourne	118 (portrait),
Bartelstone, John	8 m., 200-201, 206-209	Huthmacher, Werner, Berlin	78-81		118-121
Boardman, Brett	140-143	ICRAVE, New York	202 (portrait)	Peter Clarke Photography, Melbourne	164-167
Boora, Portland	144-147	Ivanic, Relja, Serbia	126-129	Pickering, Kate, Baran Studio Architecture	180 (portrait)
Braun, Zooey	196 (portrait), 196-199	Iwan Baan Studio	20-23	Piller, Mathew	94-97
Burgassi, Nicolò, OKNOSTUDIO, Livorno	192 a., 193-195	Jaarsma, Rogier	42-45	PL.ARCHITEKCI	152 (portrait)
Buscher, Ralf	68-71	Jacobsen, Kristine	72 (portrait)	pS Arkitektur, Stockholm	202 (portrait), 202-205
Caprarescu, Vlad	90-93	Jensen, Alan	114-117	Reaktion Eins	226-229
Carossio, Carlo	148-151	Joliet, Laure	234-237	Remond, Luc	140 (portrait), 258-261
Celander, Ulf, Göteborg	222-225	Keeney + Law Photography	176-179	Rieder, Franziska	78 (portrait)
Conder, Ryan	50 (portrait), 234 (portrait)	Knight, Travis	188-191	Rojo de la Vega, Vanessa, New York	173 (portrait)
Cristian, Corvin	90 (portrait)	Knocke, Karsten	156-159	Sanidad, Jasper	8 r., 50-55, 106 (portrait), 106-109
Cuypers, Peter	110-113	Kuszynska, Monika	152-155		184 (portrait), 184-187
Damonte, Bruce	8 l., 122-125	Lake, Candice	238-241	Seelen, Mark, Hamburg	214 (portrait), 214-217
de Wilde, Corneel	12 (portrait), 12-15	Lake, Quintain	138-139, 160-163	Stasek, Peter	76-77, 98-101
Design Blitz, San Francisco	122 (portrait)	M17 office, Moscow	254 (portrait)	TADA (YUKAI)	242-245
Designliga, München	60 (portrait), 60-63	Maksimovic, Milan, Serbia	126 (portrait)	Tsutsumi, Yoshimasa	16 (portrait)
Dlugosz, Hanna	250-253	Mandt, Roger Valentin, Berlin	134 (portrait), 134-137,	V_Confession office, Moscow	254-257
estudio ji	168 (portrait)		246 (portrait), 246-249	Weiblen, Dirk	9, 82-85
Frahm, Klaus	86-89	Milbourne, Tanja	10-11, 32-35	Williams, Adrien	56-59
Frutos, David, Murcia	168-171	Molly De	176 (portrait)	Willians, Matthew, New York	173-176
Goerke, Marcel	164 (portrait)	MOST Architecture, Rotterdam	42 (portrait)		
Guerra, Fernando	36-41	Müller, Börje	46-49	All other pictures were made available by the architects.	
Hamelin, Jimmy	56 (portrait)	Nagels, Sonya	114 (portrait)		
Hargis, Scott	180-183	nefaresearch publications, Moscow	230-233		
Haslam, Andy	218-221	Norlander, Rasmus	72-75	Cover front: Quintain Lake	
Hiromatsu, Misae (Beijing Ruijing Photo)	6, 16 m. b.,	nuvolaB, Firenze	192 (portrait), 192 b.	Cover back: left: Keeney + Law Photography	
	17-19	Onesize	24 (portrait), 24-27	right: Hanna Dlugosz	

IMPRINT

The Deutsche Nationalbibliothek lists this publication in the Deutsche Nationalbibliografie; detailed bibliographic data are available in the Internet at http://dnb.dnb.de

ISBN 978-3-03768-181-7

© 2015 by Braun Publishing AG
www.braun-publishing.ch

The work is copyright protected. Any use outside of the close boundaries of the copyright law, which has not been granted permission by the publisher, is unauthorized and liable for prosecution. This especially applies to duplications, translations, microfilming, and any saving orprocessing in electronic systems.

1st edition 2015

Editor: Sibylle Kramer
Editorial staff: María Barrera del Amo, Jakob Grelck, Helen Gührer
Translation: Geoffrey Steinherz
Graphic concept: ON Grafik | Tom Wibberenz
Layout: María Barrera del Amo
Reproduction: Bild1Druck GmbH, Berlin

All of the information in this volume has been compiled to the best of the editors' knowledge. It is based on the information provided to the publisher by the architects' and designers' offices and excludes any liability. The publisher assumes no responsibility for its accuracy or completeness as well as copyright discrepancies and refers to the specified sources (architects' and designers' offices). All rights to the photographs are property of the photographer (please refer to the picture credits).